CAPROCK
CHRONICLES

CAPROCK
CHRONICLES

MORE TALES OF THE LLANO ESTACADO

EDITED BY JOHN T. "JACK" BECKER & DAVID J. MURRAH

Introduction by Paul Carlson

THE
History
PRESS

Published by The History Press
Charleston, SC
www.historypress.com

Copyright © 2021 by John T. "Jack" Becker and David J. Murrah
All rights reserved

Front cover: Top left, public domain; center, courtesy National Ranching Heritage Center, Texas Tech University; right courtesy Christie Martinez; bottom, courtesy Aaron Lynskey. *Back cover*: Courtesy Sherry Robinson.

First published 2021

ISBN 9781467150804

Library of Congress Control Number: 2021943812

This book is dedicated to our longtime friend and colleague Paul H. Carlson, PhD, one of the most outstanding and productive historians in the nation, as well as creator of the "Caprock Chronicles" newspaper series.

CONTENTS

CONTENTS

CONTENTS

PREFACE

Which is it—Llano Estacado, Caprock or South Plains? Or, "Do you live on the Cap or off?" While the questions may not make sense to many, the thousands of residents who live along the perimeter of the Llano Estacado certainly know that the second question simply means, "Do you live on the High Plains or on the rolling plains?"

These interchangeable terms evolved over centuries. The formation that divides the High Plains from the rolling plains is the Caprock Escarpment, which marks the boundary of the Llano Estacado. The distinguished Texas historian H. Bailey Carroll, who received BA and MA degrees at Texas Tech in 1938, defines the Caprock as the "hard layer underlying the Llano Estacado...a 'hard-pan' layer that developed a few feet below the ground as highly mineral subsoil particles which cemented themselves together to form a rock-like layer that resists erosion." In essence, it is the Caprock that serves as a base for the several feet of the windswept topsoil that grow thousands of acres of cotton, corn, grain sorghum and other crops.

Due to the integral relationship of the terms "Caprock" and "Llano Estacado," Carroll also noted that "[a]lthough the name Caprock technically applies only to the formation itself, the expression is often loosely used to mean the entire region of the southern high plains."

According to another outstanding historian, H.E. Bolton, it was the Caprock escarpment that gave the Llano Estacado its name. As Spanish explorers approached the high mesa from the west, he noted, the rising

The "Caprock" refers to the escarpment at the top of the ridges that border much of the perimeter of the Llano Estacado. *Courtesy Ellen Carlson.*

Caprock reminded them of fortifications, giving the appearance of a "stockaded rampart," or "staked plains" (*llano estacado* in Spanish).

Early American visitors to the area, such as Josiah Gregg and Randolph B. Marcy, consistently referred to the treeless prairies as the Llano Estacado, and bison hunters used the term "yarner," a mispronunciation of *llano*. In all likelihood, it was the first Anglo settlers in the late 1870s who first began to use "Caprock" as a singular term to describe the region.

A few years later, another term, "South Plains," came into widespread use as land promoters and railroads in the early 1900s used the expression to advertise the region's potential for farming. In time, multiple businesses, an army air field (later Reese Air Force Base) and even a college at Levelland bore the South Plains moniker.

Until recently, the term "Llano Estacado" was rarely used except for the naming of a few businesses, most notably the Llano Estacado Winery, the founder of the region's now booming wine industry. Then, in the early 1990s, Lubbock's new mayor, David R. Langston, asked some of us to try to promote the term "Llano Estacado" as a way to call attention to the area's rich history. For a few months, we provided to the *Lubbock Avalanche-Journal* a series of articles in a column entitled "The Llano Estacado." About the same time, David Murrah had a daily radio series on Lubbock's KRFE titled *Yarns of the Llano*, telling stories about life in the region.

In 2013, the late John Miller Morris, who grew up in Amarillo and served as professor of political science and geography at the University of Texas at San Antonio, published his classic *El Llano Estacado: Exploration and Imagination on the High Plains of Texas and New Mexico, 1536–1860*. Since then, both the terms "Caprock" and "Llano Estacado" have come into more prominence, thanks to Paul Carlson's initiation of the weekly "Caprock Chronicles" series in the *Lubbock Avalanche-Journal* in 2016 and the resulting publication of two books comprising essays from that column, *Hidden History of the Llano Estacado* (2017) and *Historic Tales of the Llano Estacado* (2020).

And then there is Shelley Armitage's very personal memoir, *Walking the Llano: A Texas Memoir of Place*, published in 2017. Shelley grew up in Vega on the northern edge of the Llano Estacado, and through a series of hikes along its perimeter and adjoining canyons, she captured the idea that the land has its own memories and cycles from human occupation that "surface only for the observant, who may hear and articulate something of the image and its instant intuitions." She also added, "There is persistence in this habit of landscape, this llano lyric, if in catching the motion, you can hear the song."

Perhaps it is this persistence that continues to produce the stories the many contributors have made to the ongoing series of articles that make up the "Caprock Chronicles," and subsequently to this book. We are grateful for their interest in and devotion to the history of the Llano Estacado. We especially appreciate Paul Carlson for his insight, knowledge and assistance in this compilation. Thanks also to the staff of the Southwest Collection at Texas Tech University for their help in preserving and making available its rich resources and photos. And, as always, thanks to our spouses, Cindy Becker and Ann Murrah, for tolerating our love of history and the attention it requires.

DAVID J. MURRAH AND JOHN T. "JACK" BECKER

INTRODUCTION

The Llano Estacado is perhaps the largest mesa in North America. Located in the American Southwest, it extends across parts of western Texas and eastern New Mexico. Level to a great extent, the high plateau on three sides is situated fifty to three hundred or more feet above neighboring landforms. It is a semi-arid tableland dominated economically in 2021 by petroleum mining, cattle feeding and cotton farming.

With its huge, open and often empty range lands, the Llano Estacado appears rural and agricultural in character. But the big area is dominated by its busiest cities: Lubbock, Amarillo and the twin cities of Midland and Odessa, where urban and political activity remains conservative, as does the region's religious and moral temperament.

Historically speaking, the Llano is a young region. Despite its youth, or because of it, many of the Llano's historic leaders, ancient places and astonishing events remain unknown to the general public. In *Caprock Chronicles: More Tales of the Llano Estacado*, David J. Murrah and John T. "Jack" Becker present an exceptional collection of short historic sketches on the Llano Estacado that together describe a number of little-known personalities and events of the region's relatively short past.

The book represents the third volume in a series that reaches back to January 2016, when the *Lubbock Avalanche-Journal* began a weekly column on Llano Estacado history. As a retired professor of history at Texas Tech University, I became founding editor of a column, titled "Caprock Chronicles." With permission from both the Lubbock newspaper and the

Introduction

authors who wrote the weekly essays, David Murrah and I collected fifty-six representative columns and in late 2017 published them in *Hidden History of the Llano Estacado* with The History Press. Fortunately, the publication enjoyed both critical and material success. As a result, three years later, again with permission from the Lubbock newspaper and the authors, we prepared a second volume of "Caprock Chronicles" essays, this one titled *Historic Tales of the Llano Estacado*. An attractive, popular little collection of historic sketches, it contains forty-seven eight-hundred-word essays that range across the Llano's geologic and recent past and from the Canadian River south to the Midland-Odessa country.

Like the two previous books in the series, *Caprock Chronicles: More Tales of the Llano Estacado* covers a wide variety of topics, ranging from the deep archaeological past to the very present and written by scholars whose research interests have centered on the High Plains. Becker, who assumed editorship of the *Avalanche-Journal*'s popular "Caprock Chronicles" column in 2018, and Murrah, who has been the managing director on all three books, have assembled another unconventional but highly readable collection of short histories of the Llano Estacado. Their book, like others in the series, includes some fresh looks at old issues and some new material not published previously. Also, like other books in the series, the lively essays in this volume represent something of a history classroom made palatable by superb storytelling.

Caprock Chronicles: More Tales of the Llano Estacado—with its forty-eight essays accompanied by photos, maps or other illustrations—provides an unconventional look at the region's history and personalities. Collectively, the essays offer up an informative and delightful examination of the area's past. Because it is full of good stories and fascinating analysis, the book should be kept by the bedside lamp, the living room coffee table or the poolside lounge. Enjoy!

Paul H. Carlson

PART I

HIDDEN IN THE SAND

Sand—below and above ground on the vast Llano Estacado—has provided nature with a way to preserve treasure and to hide burials and other secrets. The vast Ogallala Aquifer is made of huge deposits of sand and gravel laid down millions of years ago, to eventually become a gigantic reservoir of water. On the surface, vast ranges of shifting sand hills, created by erosion from ancient riverbeds, have provided animals and humans alike a place of refuge for centuries.

This section provides a glimpse of the Ogallala and of one secret discovered in the sand hills. Included is a unique essay on how hurricanes have provided another source of water, as well as one on how the region's topography aided early inhabitants in killing bison without the benefit of horses or firearms.

It begins with a salute to the animals and humans who first traversed isolated Bailey County utilizing the legendary *La Pista de Agua Vida*, the "Trail of Living Water."

TRAIL OF LIVING WATER

Dolores Mosser

et's take a drive! My passion for Texas's back roads and trails began
with Sunday afternoon drives around southern Bailey County, Texas,
with my parents. We would climb in the pickup to tour local farms,
our family's ranchland at nearby Enochs or the Muleshoe Wildlife Refuge.
Consequently, driving around and learning every detail of my "backyard"
became a favorite pastime and the focus of my graduate studies at Texas
Tech University.

Many of my friends and colleagues share my love for the "Road Less
Taken." For example, two of them, Dr. Clint Chambers and Dr. Paul
Carlson, recently announced a forthcoming book on the Santa Fe Trail.
Their research focused on extension routes of the Santa Fe Trail that crossed
the northern Llano Estacado.

Many of my friends are also members of the West Texas Trail Association,
an important regional organization devoted to the research and promotion
of lesser-known routes across our region. Two local historical commissions/
museums recently created highly regarded "Historic Driving Tours."

The route of trails in the arid Southwest was based on the presence of
water. These trails, initially created by animal migration and maintained by
human use, were chains linking life-sustaining water sources. Therefore, to
understand the history of a region, one should begin by taking a closer look
at the ancient and historic springs and lakes.

While researching my isolated home area of Bailey County, I discovered an intriguing map compiled by local seventh graders in 1976. The students had taken great care to show the hydrology of the county, outlining area lakes, small creeks and the courses of the ancient Double Mountain Fork of the Brazos River, Blackwater Draw and Yellow House Draw.

The students pinpointed abandoned communities, isolated one-room schools and historic ranches—the VVN, Muleshoe, XIT, Janes, Figure 4 and the Door Key. The latter was located near the old school of Bula about five miles southeast of the Muleshoe National Wildlife Refuge, the oldest national game reserve in Texas, created in 1935.

But one has to drive the many roads of Bailey County to experience its abrupt landscape changes and to see its six salt lakes, freshwater springs, towering buttes and the sand dune belt. On a scenic overlook on Highway 214, one can see the outline of the once-deep winding canyon of Yellow House Draw—the ancient Brazos River.

Across this area lay the *La Pista de Agua Vida*, the "Trail of Living Water," so called by early Spanish explorers because travelers could find water sources at a distance of a day's travel by foot or horseback. In later years, the route was known as the Fort Sumner Wagon Road.

From where Lubbock is located to the Pecos River in New Mexico, this trail followed the path of the Brazos River's Yellow House and Blackwater Draws across Lubbock, Hale, Hockley, Lamb and Cochran Counties before entering and crossing Bailey County. The trail passed sixteen water stations in Texas and New Mexico before arriving at the Pecos River.

In 1968, the State of Texas defined ten scenic driving routes in a series of brochures, including one titled *The Plains Trail*. Its description of the landscape in southern Bailey County is intriguing: "A few miles north of the community of Enochs is an unusual feature of the plains. The highway crosses a depression stretching from southwest to northeast. The depression is a 'sink' of indefinite origin, in which are three natural rainwater lakes."

These lakes are the heart of the Muleshoe National Wildlife Refuge and provide migratory waterfowl with essential water each winter and home for the nation's largest concentration of sandhill cranes.

For years, the mystery and beauty of Bailey County remained a secret, but in 2005, the historical commissions of Hockley and Cochran Counties created the first of several "Texas' Last Frontier Ranch Tours." These annual events gave hundreds of eager visitors the opportunity to board buses and spend the day ranch-hopping and seeing heritage sites on the Trail of Living Water.

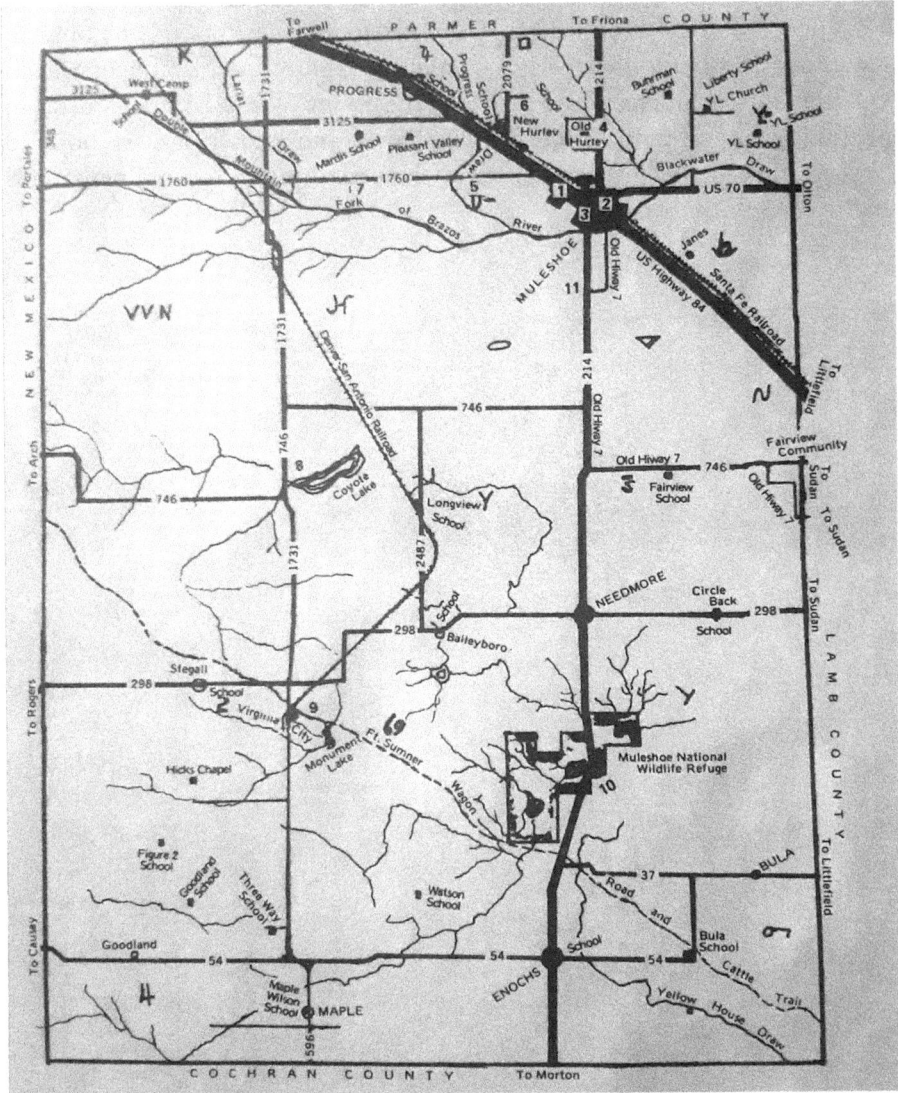

The "Trail of Living Water" is indicated as the Fort Sumner Road on the map of Bailey County, Texas. *Map from* Trails and Tales of Bailey County: The First 70 Years *and provided by Dolores Mosser.*

More recently, the Quanah Parker Trail (QPT), a recent award-winning program sponsored by the Texas Plains Trail Region of the Texas Historical Commission, has located and promoted many important Comanche camps and watering places on the trail, all designated by commemorative Quanah Parker arrows.

As dedicated trail enthusiasts, we want today's visitors to our area to appreciate the perils that early occupants, explorers and pioneers faced while crossing immense grasslands of the Llano. We take great pride in locating places of human activity. By sharing our knowledge, we hope to preserve the practice of identifying ancient roads and promote new roads that lead us to the past.

THE OGALLALA AQUIFER

Paul H. Carlson

The Ogallala Aquifer is a large underground reservoir that extends eight hundred miles through the western High Plains, from the southern edge of South Dakota to the Llano Estacado in Texas and New Mexico—eight states in all.

Its maximum width, which is in Nebraska and Wyoming, is four hundred miles. Its thickness ranges from a thin sliver to nearly one thousand feet. Early explorers commented on the springs, which emptied into water courses on top of the Caprock Escarpment and flowed out of the Llano's eastern edge. Early settlers suspected that the Caprock sat on a large aquifer but did not know how large it was.

In the 1990s, the aquifer contained about 3 billion acre-feet of groundwater, but because humans withdraw water faster than natural forces replenish it, the aquifer's water is disappearing, particularly in Texas and New Mexico.

Groundwater in the aquifer exists within voids (pore spaces) between sedimentary particles that compose the Ogallala Formation, an unconsolidated underground geologic remnant (or geologic zone) consisting of huge deposits of sand, silt, gravel and other material washed eastward from the Rocky Mountains in huge ancient rivers millions of years ago.

At one time in the ancient past, the depositional zone (the area in which the sand, silt and gravel were deposited) included much of the Great

Plains. But over millions of years, erosion on the eastern side of the Plains reduced the Ogallala Formation and its concomitant water supply, the Ogallala Aquifer.

On the western side of the Ogallala Formation, beginning about 1 million years ago, the Pecos River began to carve its crooked way north from its mouth at the Rio Grande just east of modern Langtry in Val Verde County. Over time, the Pecos lengthened, and its deepening trench and widening valley cut the head streams of the Running Water, Blackwater, Yellow House and Red River.

By the time the Pecos had reached its present extent and location, the Rocky Mountain run-off, robbed by the Pecos, could no longer replenish the Ogallala Aquifer.

In Texas and New Mexico, the aquifer underlies the flat but remarkable Llano Estacado, and through irrigation, which started in earnest after World War II, it supplies most of the water needs of the Llano's substantial agricultural economy, which includes dairying, corn and cotton growing and livestock raising.

In Nebraska, where the Ogallala Aquifer is enormous, it underlies the state's extensive Sand Hills, and as in Texas and New Mexico, it supplies most of the region's agricultural water needs through irrigation, particularly in the Sand Hills, with its new emphasis on corn growing for ethanol production.

In Texas, in a general sense, the water table of the aquifer parallels the topographic surface of the Llano Estacado. That is, water in the aquifer mainly flows west to east, but there is also a definite north–south flow.

Today, as indicated, natural recharge is insufficient to make up for withdrawals from the Ogallala Aquifer. When the Ogallala Formation and its aquifer extended west to the Rockies during the Pleistocene epoch (1.6 million years ago to 10,000 years ago), natural recharge was large, and the water table remained high. But erosion on the eastern edge and the Pecos River on the western side, as well as the onset of drier, warmer weather in the later Pleistocene (approximately 10,000 years ago), reduced the amount of recharge.

Irrigation in recent years has also affected recharge. In 2019, for example, a farmer-rancher in eastern New Mexico reported that five of his seven center-pivot well and irrigation systems could no longer pump water; the aquifer was dry below each of the five big wells. Conversely, a farmer-rancher in north-central Nebraska has not noticed a decline in the water table at any of his several center-pivot well and irrigation systems.

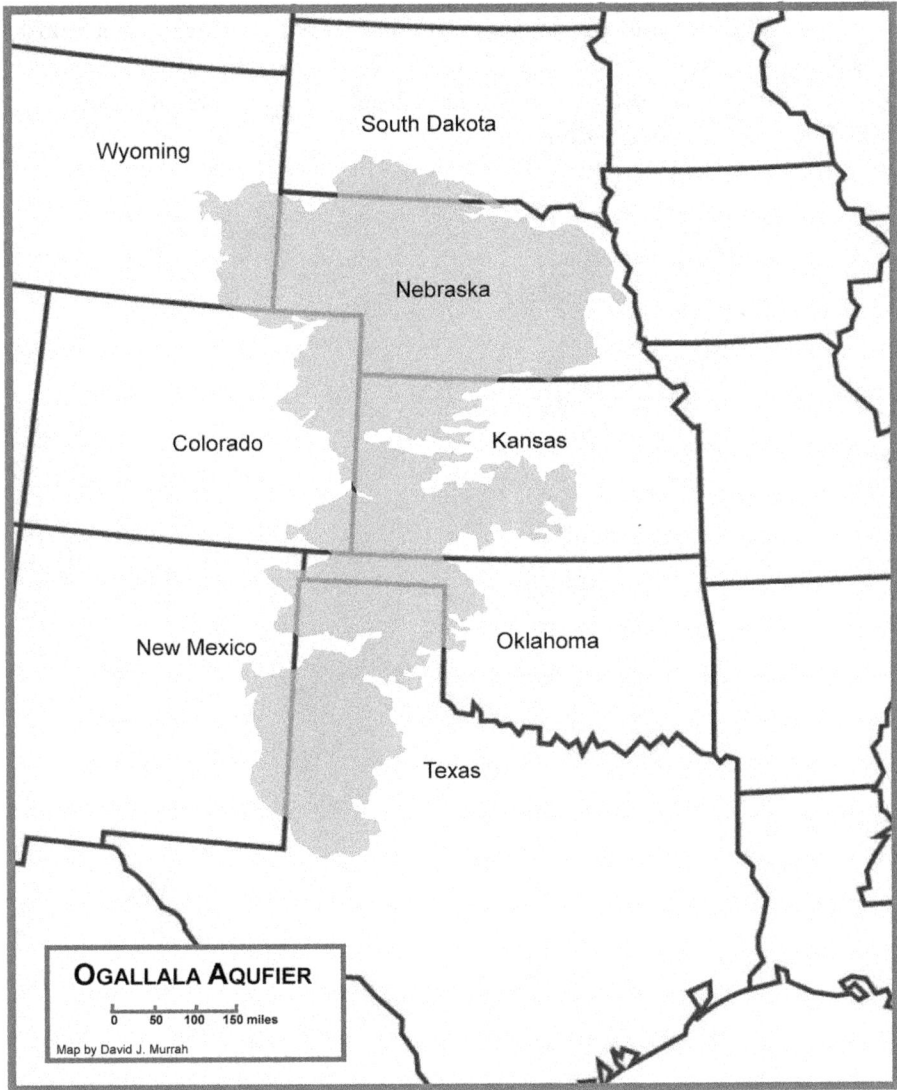

The Ogallala Aquifer provides ground water for eight different states. *Courtesy David J. Murrah.*

Nonetheless, irrigation for agricultural purposes and pumping for urban needs continues to draw down the aquifer's water supplies.

In a general sense, one might say that while a few places, such as in parts of the western Sand Hills of Nebraska, get a limited number of inches of recharge per year, the average recharge throughout the aquifer zone is less than one inch per year. The amount is not enough to sustain the aquifer.

In both the past and the present, aquifer water has proved enormously beneficial for those people who live on the Caprock. Clearly, however, continued long-term use of the Ogallala Aquifer appears troublesome and in need of major reevaluation.

THE IMPACT OF HURRICANES ON WEST TEXAS

Richard Peterson

One quick and easy way to help recharge the Ogallala Aquifer would be to harness a hurricane and let it rain out across the Llano Estacado. Over the centuries, that phenomenon has happened, but all too infrequently to be a major supplier of water.

Texas has a long and well-recognized history dealing with hurricanes. In both 1875 and 1886, the port of Indianola, where many early immigrants to Texas first set foot on the Lone Star State, was hit by devastating storms from which the town never recovered.

The 1900 Galveston hurricane yielded the largest death toll in the United States attributable to a weather event—estimates ranged between six thousand and twelve thousand. Storms in recent years, such as Harvey in 2017, have brought untold destruction to the areas between Corpus Christi to east of Houston. These storms all came in from the Gulf of Mexico.

These Atlantic storms generally have only an indirect effect on the High Plains. The largest storms may have an extensive cloud shield, which can spread over the High Plains.

Hurricane Gilbert (1988), one of the strongest Atlantic storms on record, made landfall south of Brownsville and maintained vigorous organization northwestward to the Big Bend area. Lubbock was under its cloud shield, while from the ground clear skies could be seen to the west.

For West Texas, the hurricanes that have an important impact come from the Northeast Tropical Pacific Ocean (NETROPAC). Until the mid-twentieth century, there was great ignorance about tropical storm occurrence in this region. Detection of tropical storms in the area has waxed and waned.

During the California Gold Rush, ships carrying prospectors around Cape Horn and up the western coast of the Americas undoubtedly encountered tropical storms. Nevertheless, scientific papers on the worldwide distribution of hurricane-like storms omitted the NETROPAC.

In the first half of the twentieth century, tuna fishing fleets provided weather observations off the West Coast; however, cost-cutting led to elimination of radio equipment on the boats. In the 1960s, weather satellites came online, leading to more routine detection of the tropical developments.

The eastern Pacific Ocean from the Central America up to Mexico spawns the greatest number of tropical storms and hurricanes in the Western Hemisphere. Worldwide, only the Northwest Pacific Ocean is more prolific, where the strongest storms there are called typhoons.

Even now, for the most part, the NETROPAC storms receive little attention. Usually they travel to the northwest, away from the continent, and dissipate over colder water. Occasionally one will threaten the Hawaiian Islands. Toward October, however, tropical storms may get caught by strengthening weather patterns over North America, causing them to curve to the northeast and inland. The western regions of Mexico bear the brunt of the high winds and flooding.

As a storm is carried northeastward, its lower-level circulation is disrupted by the central mountains of Mexico. Nevertheless, the upper circulation and copious amounts of moist air can reach West Texas. Hurricane Tico in October 1983 was a prime example of what can develop. The Category 4 hurricane turned to the northwest near Mazatlán, Mexico. In Mexico, there was extensive flooding and damage; at least 134 deaths were recorded. As the storm remnants emerged east of the mountains of Mexico, they were met by a cold front coming across the Texas Panhandle from the north.

While the core of the storm was still over the higher terrain of Mexico and before the front had arrived in Lubbock, rain began to fall beneath the outer reaches of the storm. The result was record rain from northeastern Oklahoma into West Texas. Over a five-day period, Lubbock measured 8.67 inches of rain, with 5.82 inches falling on October 19 alone.

The city's playa lakes spilled water into the streets. Leroy Elmore Park flooded and blocked Quaker Avenue for weeks. The four lanes of traffic were diverted into the neighborhood to the west. There was prolonged disruption

September 8, 2008, brought record rainfall to Lubbock, the most received in twenty-four hours. *From weather.gov.*

of traffic due to the street flooding. Two years earlier, another NETROPAC hurricane named Norma dumped twenty inches of rain north of Abilene.

The formation of tropical storms is extremely dependent on ocean temperatures. Due to global weather patterns across the whole of the Pacific Ocean, there are periods when the temperatures of the NETROPAC are above the long-term average (El Niño) and periods when they are cooler (La Niña).

These variations occur over several years and are sporadic rather than periodic. When El Niño conditions prevail, a greater number of tropical storms form off the west coast of Central America. In general, the South Plains receives more precipitation during El Niño events.

Not every hurricane season has storms that curve and cross Mexico. However, over the last thirty years, there have been one or two per year. Even if the storm remains to the west, its moisture can greatly affect the South Plains.

During September 9–13, 2008, Tropical Storm Lowell fed the formation of heavy rains in the Lubbock area. The all-time twenty-four-hour rainfall record for Lubbock was set at 7.80 inches, closing schools, blocking streets and flooding homes and businesses.

Long-term climatology data shows that West Texas get its moisture from a bimodal distribution of precipitation—the maximum falls in the late spring and in the fall, the latter in part due to NETROPAC storm moisture.

THE PLAINVIEW BISON KILL SITE

Paul H. Carlson

There is an ancient bison kill site near downtown Plainview, Texas. Now buried under layers of debris (once a garbage dump), it is located in a gentle curve of Running Water Draw, the once-impressive watercourse that forms the upper reaches of White River.

Historical and archaeological information for the site remains difficult to pin down, associated with controversy and disagreement and often presented in jargon-rich prose understood only by geoarchaeologists, paleontologists and related Paleoindian specialists.

Archaeological evidence at the site suggests that late Paleoindian people, about ten thousand years ago, used the site at least twice a year (once in the fall and once in the spring) and maybe other times as well. The ancient hunters either drove a now-extinct species of bison (*Bison antiquus*), which stood about a third larger than modern bison, over a small, steep cliff at the site or trapped the large mammals in a marshy section of Running Water Draw, then a meandering but perennial stream.

Discovery of the site dates to the late 1930s and early 1940s, when a local company began mining caliche from the draw. In the resulting quarry and its tailings, Plainview-area residents found and collected stone projectile (spear) points and related artifacts, some scattered through the wide and shallow but once deep draw.

The news brought in professional archaeologists, who visited the site in 1944. Later, beginning in the summer of 1945—June through October—the archaeologist, through systematic excavation, discovered a large bone bed that contained partial skeletons of more than one hundred bison.

They also found at least twenty-eight projectile points (some refashioned into butchering knives) and, according to Vance T. Holliday, "a few amorphous flake tools." E.A. Sellards, director of the Bureau of Economic Geology, and the Texas Memorial Museum of the University of Texas led scientists at the Plainview "dig." His chief assistant and close collaborator, geologist Glen L. Evans, guided much of the field work at the site (originally called "Locality 8"), and Grayson E. Meade, a vertebrate paleontologist with Texas Technological College (Texas Tech University), joined the team.

The Sellards team dug pits in Running Water Draw and along the draw's walls. They wanted to study the site's stratigraphy and, of course, examine the bone bed. In his subsequent report of the Plainview site, Sellards described the bone area as "a mat of closely spaced, disarticulated bones and skeletons…of approximately 100 bison…in an area of about 500 square feet" with "an average thickness of scarcely a foot." And as Holliday and others have noted, "an unknown number of artifacts probably were removed by collectors."

As indicated, the Sellards team collected plenty of animal bones and other significant lithic artifacts, but it found no bison skulls or tailbones, suggesting that the people who used the Plainview kill site removed the heads, hides and tailbones intact, likely for processing elsewhere.

The hunters may have saved the skulls for religious purposes. Or, in some cases, they may have cracked open the skulls to use the brains during hide tanning. After taking from the site a portion of the skeleton assembly in 1945, the Sellards team returned four years later in November 1949 and removed another key section of the principal bone bed.

Significantly, Sellards and his team realized that their projectile points differed from earlier Clovis and Folsom (Paleoindian) stone weapons. The Plainview (late Paleoindian) points occurred lanceolate in shape or structure—that is, without the fluting or grooving as existed in earlier projectile styles.

Moreover, according to Holliday, the Plainview site contained "the largest collection of lanceolate points, in the region, found in place." Partly as a result of the different point patterns, scientists noted a change in cultural traditions beginning around 10,000 years ago and dubbed it the Plainview complex or culture to distinguish it from the earlier Clovis (circa 11,500

This statue of *Bison antiquus* at the Lubbock Lake National Historic Landmark is one and a half times bigger that modern bison and is typical of the animals hunted at the Plainview site. *Courtesy Jack Becker.*

to 11,000 years ago) and Folsom (circa 10,800 to 10,300 year ago) life patterns. Additional pits along the draw provided important geological and stratigraphic information, including a shift toward a drier, warmer climate.

Beginning in the 1970s, the use of the site as a dump covered the area, ruining some or any further use to scientists. Nonetheless, in 1977, Eddie Guffee, associated with the Wayland Baptist University Archaeological Research Laboratory, found some of the old bone bed intact, but not before removing nine feet of garbage and other debris. The location has not been investigated systematically in nearly forty years.

Still, because of what it reveals about shifting life patterns, bison evolution and environmental transformations, the Plainview bison kill site remains significant. The bones, stone points and other lithic material suggest a Plainview culture that represents the divide between Paleoindian times and the Archaic period that followed.

ANOTHER BISON KILL SITE

Gene Lynskey

In the previous article by Paul Carlson about an ancient bison kill site at Plainview, he noted that "ancient hunters either drove a now-extinct species of bison (*Bison antiquus*), which stood about a third larger than modern bison, over a small, steep cliff at the site or trapped the large mammals in a marshy section of Running Water Draw, then a meandering but perennial stream."

It's hard to imagine there being a "steep cliff" at the site of Plainview, and my guess would be that hunters would catch bison in the marshy mud of the draw to make their kill. Apparently, the process worked similarly at other kill sites, such as Lubbock Lake and at Coyote Lake in Bailey County near Muleshoe.

Dr. Carlson's account reminded me of a story told to me by my great-uncle Malcolm Sanders one day when I was a teenager in the 1970s. It was about my grandfather's discovery of a bison kill site. He took me to the site by driving north out of Slaton on a county road that meandered down the south rim of a canyon and crossed a narrow bridge over the river.

He first showed me the shelter that he and his brother, my grandfather Courtney Sanders, constructed as kids in the 1930s, made from old cedar posts and wooden plank walls. Then, as we started up the north rim, we drove through a dense canopy of elm trees that Uncle Malcolm said came as seedlings from the Sanders homeplace near downtown Slaton. After passing through the trees, he pointed to the left to a box canyon, where he said Courtney had discovered multiple piles of bison skulls in the late 1920s.

My best guess is that Courtney made the find in about 1928 at age fourteen or fifteen, when he had the opportunity to explore the isolated canyons at will. He would pretend to head to school from his home in Slaton but instead would strike out for the canyons, a three-and-a-half-mile walk. One day, his mother, Edith Sanders, met his teacher at their grocery store and asked how Courtney was doing in school, and the teacher responded, "I don't know. I haven't seen him in months!"

Courtney explored the canyons and found the piles of bison skulls and bones in the bottom of a box canyon. It was an apparent kill site, and the location was the bottom of a sharp three-hundred-foot drop-off from the rim above. Before Courtney went into the U.S. Navy in 1933, he took Malcolm—who was about seven years old—to see the skull piles.

According to Dr. Carlson in his book *Deep Time*, Folsom-era hunters may have used herding methods to edge bison into a box canyon, or they used a "jump-kill" method that forced animals over a cliff, counting on the fall to either cripple or kill them for easy butchering. "This method," he wrote, "continued to be used on the Great Plains until modern times." Apparently, this site north of Slaton may have been one used well into the nineteenth century. According to my grandfather, the skulls he found were contemporary bison and not those of the Paleo era.

After returning home from the navy in 1936, Courtney married Vivian Teague and worked for his father in the grocery business in Slaton and Post; then he worked in Corpus Christi during World War II. After the war, he relocated to Morton, where he later established Sanders Fertilizer and Chemical.

But he never lost his love for finding ancient artifacts and became an avid arrowhead hunter. His favorite time was always in the spring after sand storms. He was the only one in town with a big smile on his face while the sand was blowing because he knew that the erosion would expose buried points. I was the same way—it was from him that I learned how to hunt for points, and it remains my very favorite thing to do.

Meanwhile, Uncle Malcolm, strongly influenced by his best friend and my cousin F. Earl Green, chose to study geology at Texas Tech, and in 1951, he wrote his master's thesis on the sand hills of Bailey County, while Earl studied the sand hills of Lamb and Hale Counties. Eleven years later, in 1962, my cousin Earl led a team that excavated the Blackwater Draw site near Portales, New Mexico, which provided new evidence on Folsom and

This sharp drop-off from the level plain into the canyon below was a perfect location for Native Americans to drive bison over the cliff. *Courtesy Aaron Lynskey.*

Clovis cultures in archaeological studies. Earl Green later became director of the Texas Tech Museum before beginning a long career with the Texas Parks and Wildlife Department. He is memorialized at the Blackwater Draw Museum at Portales. He also documented the discovery of the Arch Lake Woman, as referenced in the next essay.

My grandfather Courtney Sanders died in 1997 and Uncle Malcolm in 2005. I shall always be grateful to them for instilling in me a love for the High Plains and the windswept sand dunes that have been a home for humans for more than ten thousand years.

HIDDEN IN THE SAND

Gene Lynskey

In the previous article, I told the story of my grandfather's discovery of a bison kill site near Slaton. His stories led me to begin exploring the country around where we farmed in southern Cochran County and ultimately led to my greatest find, a discovery that still haunts me to this day.

Not far away from our farm in southern Cochran County lay the remnants of the Mescalero sand dunes in northern Yoakum County. While most of the terrain had been disturbed by farming, there were still active dunes that shifted with the wind. In the midst of them, I had a favorite place to hunt for Indian artifacts.

I had spotted this area from miles away; it stood out because it had a different stand of grass, and its unusual color led me to it. The presence of burned rock and flint chips on the surface implied that it had been a campsite. That day, my dad, the late Don Lynskey, and I found several points. Also, there was so much camp debris exposed by wind erosion that I not only filled my pockets but also had to use my shirttail to hold all the flint and stone tools. It must have been an area that had not been discovered by artifact hunters before.

On my birthday in October 1997—I always went back to the site on my birthday as my special treat to myself—I found a few points. About a month later, we had our big, seemingly annual Thanksgiving week sandstorm, and I decided to check out the site again. This time, when I came around a dune, from a distance, I could see bones, which I first presumed were deer remains. I walked over to see if there were any antlers, but much to my surprise, it was a human skeleton recently exposed by wind erosion.

At first, I didn't know what to do other than take off my cap as a matter of reverence for the dead, give a prayer and then walk away. My first thought was that the skeleton was that of a Native American. However, because it appeared to be in such good shape, I worried that it might be that of a woman who had been missing in the area for some time, and so I reported the find to the Yoakum County Sheriff's Office.

Anthropologists from the Forensic Anthropology Lab at Texas Tech University came to help determine whether the skeleton was modern or ancient. I insisted that if the find were that of a Native American, the bones should eventually be reburied at the site. They agreed and then documented and collected the skeleton, taking it to the lab at Tech. Their findings confirmed that the skeleton was Native American, but I was shocked to learn that that it was Archaic and approximately three thousand years old!

Their research also concluded that the skeleton was that of a woman who was approximately twenty-five to thirty-five years old at the time of her death. She had suffered from arthritis, starvation at numerous times

Anthropologist Kent Hicks at the skeleton discovery site in Yoakum County in 1997. *Courtesy Patrick Lewis.*

The remains of the skeleton that was buried in the sand. *Courtesy Patrick Lewis.*

and had extensive teeth decay. While the cause of her demise could not be determined, they indicated that she had been deliberately buried, placed in a fetal position on her right side, her face facing north.

The researchers concluded that the burial was significant "specifically because there is a lack of archaic period skeletal remains on the southern plains of west Texas." Their report, written by Robert Paine and Patrick Lewis and entitled "An Archaic Human Burial from Yoakum County, Texas: The Crossroads of Bioarchaeology and Forensic Anthropology," was published by the Texas Academy of Science (and is available at thefreelibrary.com).

But what the report does not say is why the skeleton was still relatively well preserved late in the twentieth century when I found it. I think that, at the time of her death, she was probably buried on the east side of the dune, but by the time I found her three thousand years later, the dune had shifted across her grave and left her exposed on the windward side. Also, because she was buried a few inches above the clay, her body was never in moisture for any length of time and therefore did not deteriorate as it would have otherwise.

The report does indicate that the Archaic hunters and gatherers experienced "a very physically demanding way of life." I have lived most of my life within a few miles of that sand dune and know how difficult it is to make a living in this area, but one can only imagine the struggles and challenges the Archaic people had, armed only with small spears.

To the best of my knowledge, there has been only one other Native American burial site documented in Yoakum County—that of a child who had died in the 1870s. My discovery compares more to that of the Arch Lake Woman, discovered in Roosevelt County, New Mexico, in 1967 and documented by my cousin F. Earl Green, who was then director of the Texas Tech Museum. Tests later determined that she had lived ten thousand years ago, making her the third-oldest human remains found in North America.

I still have mixed feelings about my find. I felt guilty for intruding on her sacred burial place. At the time, had I known for sure that the remains were of a Native American woman, I would probably have just reburied her. But after learning that such finds are extremely rare, that she was from the late Archaic period and that she has been returned to the site, I am glad to have been a part of the discovery of an amazing story of our prehistoric times.

PART II

PRAIRIE APACHES AND COMANCHES

In 1863, the U.S. government interred both Navajo and Mescalero Apaches on the Bosque Redondo Reservation along the Pecos River below Fort Sumner, on the extreme western edge of the Llano Estacado. Supplies came from the from the east, and wagon trains cut new trails across the upper Texas Panhandle, creating new divisions of the Santa Fe Trail.

The Llano Estacado served as a major hunting ground for Comanches and Kiowas, but in 1874, Ranald Mackenzie and the U.S. Calvary routed them from the region; the following year, they persuaded Quanah Parker and his band to give up their historic home. The void left attracted Lipan Apaches in a short-lived return to their old hunting grounds. The stories of Comanches and Apaches on the Llano, along with essays about two natural lakes that were essential to the native tribes, compose this chapter.

TEXAS PANHANDLE BRANCHES
OF THE SANTA FE TRAIL

Clint E. Chambers

Modern maps of the Santa Fe Trail nearly always show two branches of the historic trail from Kansas City to Santa Fe. Both routes left Kansas City, moved southwest and struck the Arkansas River just upstream from present-day Dodge City, Kansas.

From there, the routes divided. The Cimarron Route crossed the Arkansas and moved southwest through southern Kansas, the Oklahoma Panhandle and then into New Mexico. The Mountain route followed the Arkansas River to Bent's Fort in present-day Colorado, turned southwest and climbed through Raton Pass and into New Mexico. The branches rejoined at La Junta (modern Watrous) and followed the same track into Santa Fe.

In 1863, Santa Fe traders developed two new but temporary branches, which traversed the Texas Panhandle and cut about two hundred miles off the distance between Kansas City and the newly established Bosque Redondo Reservation at Fort Sumner, New Mexico.

Bosque Redondo had been established as a reserve for captured Apaches and Navajos after the end of the Navajo War. The federal government needed to supply them with food, equipment, clothes and other goods. With about nine thousand Navajos and Apaches to feed, and not enough food crops grown in New Mexico to feed them, the government hired freighting contractors to supply the Indians' needs, and so the shorter paths quickly developed.

From near future Dodge City, the united Panhandle branches crossed the Arkansas River and followed Crooked Creek in southwestern Kansas, crossed the Cimarron River and moved to the Beaver River in what is today the Panhandle of Oklahoma.

Here the Crooked Creek branch crossed the Beaver, moved south, waded through the head of Wolf Creek in the Texas Panhandle and continued south to Adobe Walls on the north side of the Canadian River. From Adobe Walls, the trail tracked west to Atascosa, crossed to the south side of the Canadian and followed the river to Fort Bascom (established in 1863), located about forty miles north of Bosque Redondo.

The Palo Duro branch, rather than crossing the Beaver River, separated from the Crooked Creek branch, moved west up the Beaver and crossed it at the junction of Palo Duro Creek, which entered the south side of the Beaver River. It followed the Palo Duro Creek in present-day Hansford County (not to be confused with Palo Duro Canyon), southwest through the Texas Panhandle before turning west to stay on the north side of the Canadian for a distance and then crossing the big river to cut toward Fort Bascom.

From Fort Bascom, traders moved either west to Gallinas Springs on the Pecos River and eventually Santa Fe or south to Fort Sumner and Bosque Redondo.

Short-lived Fort Bascom had been established to guard Santa Fe caravans crossing through the Texas Panhandle. Soldiers at the fort kept a check on Comancheros (Hispanic-Pueblo traders who operated on the Plains) and Plains Indians.

At the newly established Fort Bascom, wagon trains bound for the United States combined, and the government provided them with a military escort to Fort Larned, Kansas, located north of the Arkansas River. Soldiers also accompanied caravans bound from Larned to Bascom.

Each year, the Texas Panhandle branches carried tons of foodstuffs, especially corn and wheat, to Bosque Redondo. But it was not enough food to keep the Indians properly nourished, and the reservation was too arid to allow Navajos to successfully grow their own crops.

The reservation was inadequate in nearly every way. Apaches departed about the time the Navajos arrived (late 1863), and the Navajos suffered from the terrible conditions.

In 1868, the government closed Bosque Redondo, and the huge wagon trains of supplies from the northeast were no longer needed. Navajos returned to their traditional homelands in northwestern New Mexico and northeastern Arizona, where they rebuilt their lives. The Texas Panhandle branches of the Santa Fe Trail, however, were not neglected. They became important in what has been called a "wagon road economy" between the Panhandle and Dodge City.

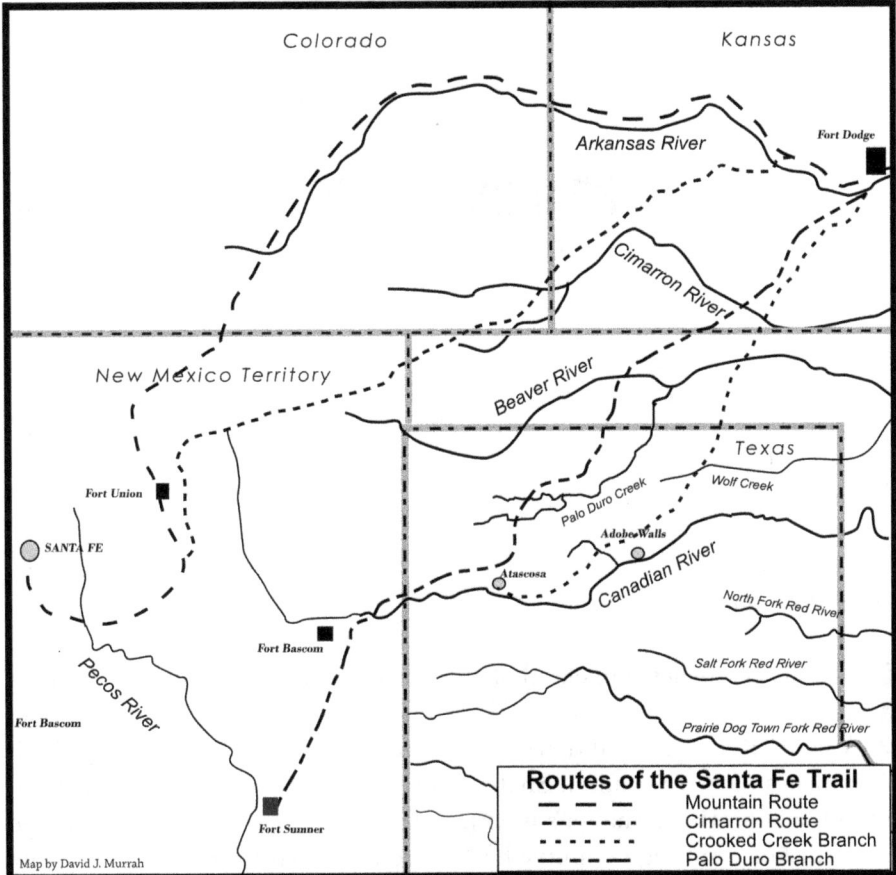

This map illustrates the two main routes of the Santa Fe Trail—the mountain route that traversed Raton Pass and the Cimarron Cutoff—as well as two alternate roads that crossed the upper Texas Panhandle. *Map courtesy David J. Murrah.*

Buffalo hunters in the 1870s made good use of the well-marked routes, and in the 1880s, cattlemen likewise used them to trail livestock to Dodge City. From 1863 to 1867, Jack Stilwell, when a teenager, served as a Teamster on the Texas Panhandle branches, but he also worked the other Santa Fe trails, spending winters in Santa Fe and traveling between Santa Fe and Kansas City twice a year. In 1893, he recalled, "Freighters discussed every route as which was better, shorter, more convenient and above all safest from Indians." When a wagon train was bound from Kansas to Bosque Redondo, he suggested, the little-known Texas Panhandle branches of the Santa Fe Trail were best.

PRAIRIE APACHES

Sherry Robinson

I n 1875, the treeless tableland of the Staked Plains was "a country almost entirely unknown except to Indians," observed Lieutenant Colonel William R. Shafter, and he wanted to explore it. With the Quahadi Comanches on a reservation, Shafter could concentrate on scouting. For the second half of 1875, Shafter's men traveled thousands of miles, "nearly the whole distance through country heretofore unknown to troops." They saw few Indians and killed only one. Of greater military importance were the trails and water holes they discovered and mapped.

The absence of the Comanches was also an invitation to Apaches, who had once lived on the Llano Estacado, and before long, a thousand Apaches, previously unknown to the army, were scattered over the region. Buffalo herds were thin, but the short buffalo grass still supported plenty of antelope.

In July 1875, Shafter led four companies of the Tenth, a detachment of Seminole scouts and seven Tonkawa scouts from Fort Concho toward the Llano Estacado and soon found signs of a large party of Indians moving west. In the sand hills, they found fresh signs of a small hunting party and a trail, five or six days old, leading north to some water holes, where about three hundred people and hundreds of horses and mules had camped. The Apaches were apparently in no hurry to leave and didn't try to hide their trail, "which could have been followed at a gallop by moonlight," Shafter wrote.

A New Mexico scenic marker with the Llano Estacado in the background, once the homeland of the Prairie Apaches. *Courtesy Sherry Robinson.*

Soldiers then found the bodies of a woman and her days-old infant lying dead at her breast. They followed the trail to the Pecos and then north. At 1:00 a.m., a party of twenty or thirty warriors crossing back on the trail ran into one company of soldiers, and they exchanged fire. The raiders hurried back to warn their people.

The next morning, Shafter took the trail with forty-five of the best mounted men. After twenty miles, he found the camp the Apaches had left that morning, located at a sizable spring with enough water for thousands of horses. They apparently planned to make this a permanent camp. Soldiers spent the next day burning lodges and lodge poles. Most of the Indians had ridden west and scattered. Shafter predicted that they wouldn't go into Fort Stanton in New Mexico but would remain on the plains to hunt bison, "in which event, I hope to get them yet," he wrote.

On October 18, troops attacked a camp at *Laguna Sabinas* (Cedar Lake), a salt lake near present Seminole, and captured twenty-five horses and mules. They destroyed fifty sacks of mesquite beans, three or four thousand pounds of bison meat, about one hundred undressed hides, one hundred lodge poles and cooking utensils. Soldiers found that they could reach good water by digging anywhere near the edge of the lake, and the grass was excellent. Mesquite roots provided plenty of wood.

From there, Lieutenant Andrew Geddes, of the Twenty-Fifth Infantry, followed the trail south to the Rio Grande. About sixty miles above the mouth of the Pecos at Shafter Crossing, his men discovered a fine spring. "From this spring to Howard's wells and the Pecos country has never been scouted," Shafter wrote. "From this point [Howard's Well] west to the Rio Grande the country is least known of any in this Department and is the most difficult to scout in." Deep, rocky ravines obstructed wagons, and cactus, especially the aptly named Spanish dagger, made travel painful for horses. "There is undoubtedly plenty of water and this country has always been a favorite resort for the Apaches and Lipans."

Officers writing reports often made references simply to "Apaches," rather than to Mescaleros or Lipans, because a great many Apaches were unknown to them. One large group, called Llaneros by the Spanish, was related to the Mescaleros and Lipans.

Shafter followed a large trail to what he called the White Sand Hills (Monahans Sandhills). Shaped by the wind into mounds, bowls and slopes as ribbed as a washboard, the sands were forbidding to man and horse. Devoid of vegetation and almost impassable, they looked from a distance like snow-covered hills. They were five miles wide and twenty-five miles long, from northwest to southeast. During each of three visits, Shafter found water in almost unlimited quantities by digging two to four feet in the small depressions at the base of the hills. There were also large willows and cottonwoods that signaled water below. They didn't overtake the Apaches but did find a large lake of permanent water.

In December, nearly four hundred emaciated Apaches arrived at Fort Stanton in New Mexico. Shafter was satisfied that there wasn't "an Indian east of the Pecos and south of Red River." His assumption turned out to be premature.

LIPAN APACHES ON THE LLANO ESTACADO

Sherry Robinson

For three hundred years or more, Apaches roamed the Llano Estacado freely before surrendering the region to Comanches in the early 1700s. But they continued to make intrusions onto the plains, especially along its borders.

Lipan Apaches roamed from the Staked Plains to the Pecos, the Guadalupe Mountains and the mountains of Mexico. After 1876, however, soldiers and Texas Rangers were always on their trail.

Sometimes the Lipans were raiding. Sometimes they were just trying to reach safety, stealing a few horses here and there for their own use and butchering a cow for food. They formed small groups, or maybe two or three small groups combined. They cut telegraph lines and took the wire with them. They doubled back over their own tracks to confuse their pursuers, passed through the roughest escarpments and watched as troops lost their trail in the rocks. They stole undetected around army camps.

If they could remain in a place long enough, they made jerky, tanned skins and baked mescal. Better known as agave, or century plant, mescal was an Apache staple. They collected the plant, cut off the leaves and baked the head in a pit. The mass could be eaten right away, which tasted a bit like sweet potatoes, or it could be sliced and dried.

General Edward O.C. Ord, commander of the Department of Texas, exhorted his officers to spare "neither men nor animals" to punish or destroy the Apaches, but near constant patrols found little to report. More often than not, they chased rumors and spurious reports by freighters wanting protection or farmers hoping to sell supplies to the army.

From September 1878 to September 1879, 128 patrols from thirteen Texas posts scouted 40,100 miles and fought just two engagements. They did, however, become better acquainted with Apache geography, and their reports provide the first clear picture of Apache routes, water holes and landmarks on the Llano and surrounding area.

In a typical patrol early in 1879, Lieutenant John L. Bullis—with fifteen soldiers, twelve packers, thirty-nine Black Seminole and three Lipan scouts—trailed a group of Apaches traveling with women and children. They traced the Apaches in a wide loop from Independence Creek south of present-day Sheffield northeast to Castle Gap and on to the White Sand Hills, Horsehead Crossing on the Pecos, Antelope Wells in present Presidio County and the Guadalupes. There they filled a spring with brush and stones, which delayed the thirsty troops, who invested hours cleaning it out. Their journey's end was the Mescalero reservation in New Mexico, where Lipan and other Plains Apaches often took refuge.

The Monahans Sandhills in Ward and Winkler Counties were a part of the Prairie Apache homeland. *Courtesy Sherry Robinson.*

Later that year, Captain G.W. Arrington of the Texas Rangers' Frontier Battalion followed raiders coming from the west to strike cattle ranches along the headwaters of the Brazos, the Colorado and Concho. On December 29, 1879, the Rangers picked up a trail of raiders just past the mouth of Yellow House Canyon, a broad gap in the Caprock near present Lubbock, and followed it over rim rock toward spring-fed Tahoka Lake in present Lynn County, a favorite destination of raiders.

Later, they found a ranch cow, cut open with its paunch removed and emptied to be used as a canteen, which signaled to the Rangers that a long desert ride was soon to follow. From Tahoka, they followed the trail seven miles northwest to Double Lakes, the last known water before entering the Staked Plains.

Farther west, they plunged into white sand hills (probably the Lea-Yoakum Sand Hills), which Ranger J.B. Gibson called "the most complete picture of perfect desolation I had ever beheld." Taunted by mirages, they finally reached a real lake, where they found horse bones and the ashes of four or five campfires.

At other lakes along the trail, they found indications of a sizable camp. By this time, they were about 135 miles from their last known point and well into New Mexico. Knowing that they couldn't afford to mount an attack, the Rangers retraced their steps to one of the lakes and waited for the Apaches to appear.

While they waited, a few men went out to hunt antelope and instead found Apaches. First, the raiders tried unsuccessfully to take the Rangers' horses, and then, with guns lying across their saddles, they formed a line of battle. Each side studied the other through field glasses.

"We had often heard," one Ranger remembered, "of the desperate fighting qualities of the Apache Indians and we fully expected them, on account of their superior number, to attack us, and we prepared to give them one warm reception, and thus we stood and glared at each other for at least half an hour, but instead of them attacking us as we expected, they turned about and deliberately rode away."

The Apaches undoubtedly had a similar conversation and decided that it was not a good day to die.

CEDAR LAKE

Paul H. Carlson

Cedar Lake lies in northeast Gaines County. The largest playa on the Llano Estado, it includes some fifty-seven miles of shoreline and is named for the cedar scrubs in the area. The salty lake has served humans and animals for thousands of years.

Although its water is brackish, both ancient and modern people, according to an 1875 military report, could find "plenty of good water in numerous wells or rather dug springs in a ravine at the north end, and several large wells at the south end."

Several years ago, Ruth Hunt wrote of the large, shallow, alkali body of water: Cedar Lake "is hidden away and almost unknown to today's generation....Its barrenness is beautiful. Its view brings one to deep thought and wonder....Its...shoreline with silver...mirages...kindle the imagination."

Cedar Lake (or *Laguna Sabinas* to early Spanish explorers) has witnessed some remarkable events. Mass burial grounds exist, one each on the north and west sides, and at least two Indian cemeteries sit nearby.

Lipan Apaches and various Comanche divisions used the lake. Comanches, between about 1780 and 1880, traded at the lake with Comancheros, the New Mexico villagers who carried goods east on two-wheeled carts from the Pecos River Valley to swap their wares with Indians for bison hides and meat, stolen cattle and possibly humans.

Some writers insist—probably incorrectly—that Cynthia Ann Parker, having been taken captive by Comanches some years earlier, gave birth in

Cedar Lake looking toward the southeast. *Courtesy by Jack Becker.*

about 1850 to her son Quanah at or near Cedar Lake. Quanah became a wealthy and highly successful Comanche leader.

The U.S. Army used the lake, especially in the 1870s, as it forced Comanches to return to their reservation in the aftermath of the Texas Panhandle's 1874–75 Red River War. In fact, Lieutenant Colonel William R. Shafter in 1875 led men of his Twenty-Fourth Infantry and the Tenth Cavalry, made up almost entirely of African American Buffalo Soldiers, on a six-month-long expedition on the southern and central Llano Estacado. They found few Indians, but one of Shafter's subalterns, Lieutenant John L. Bullis, discovered a large band of Apaches at Cedar Lake. Bullis gave chase but without success in catching the fleeing Indians.

Bison hunters also used Cedar Lake. Charles A. Siringo, a cowboy detective of no little note, passed by Cedar Lake in the late 1870s and noticed bison-hide hunter "camps black with genuine buffalo hides." In 1882, near the end of the great bison hunt, George Causey, one of the most successful hide hunters, killed two hundred bison near the lake.

C.C. Slaughter, one of Texas's most prosperous cattlemen and bankers, ran the northwestern boundary of his huge Long S Ranch adjacent to Cedar

Lake. The ranch, which was about fifty miles north–south and fifty miles east–west, may have been in size second only to the famous XIT. Shortly after 1900, Slaughter reduced his Long S to about 250,000 acres, and a rancher named Fish leased thousands of acres in the Cedar Lake region. The land became the Fish Ranch. Not long afterward, J.H. Belcher and his sons, through lease and purchase, secured 111 sections in what was now called "Cedar Lake Country."

As Belcher's leases ran out, farmer-stockmen and other settlers began to acquire smaller tracts, and the population in the Cedar Lake Country increased. Mail came from Lamesa in Dawson County in mule-drawn carts, and a post office building appeared in 1907 at a place called Blue Goose (modern Loop, Texas).

In the 1920s, cotton growers turned much of the grass-covered prairie land into farms. Eventually, irrigated fields covered much of Gaines County north and west of Cedar Lake, and in 1935, petroleum wildcatters brought in the first productive oil well in the area.

The *New Handbook of Texas* notes that in "1936 the Texas Centennial Commission placed a historical marker at the north end of Cedar Lake." Among other things, the marker indicated that Quanah Parker was born nearby.

By the end of the 1930s, a town called Cedar Lake had appeared on the northeast corner of the lake. Gus White of Dawson County established the municipality on his ranchland in December 1939, shortly after citizens of his governmental precinct voted to sell beer. The village, which became known as White City, once boasted "of a lumber yard, grocery store, barber shop, four or five bars, two dance halls, an out-door dance pavilion and a two-story hotel and café." It got a post office in 1941. After World War II, when citizens voted to abolish the sale of beer, the town began to decline. By the late 1950s, "not even the post office remained."

Today, oil well pump jacks dominate an isolated, shimmery-surfaced Cedar Lake.

TAHOKA LAKE

Austin Allison

L ynn County and the lakes within its boundaries comprise one of the seminal locations on the Llano Estacado. Located in the northeastern quadrant of the county, Tahoka Lake and the springs surrounding it was a common watering hole for different populations throughout recorded history. Part of the lake's attraction was that it was a freshwater lake, usually full year-round in an area where alkali lakes and playas annually dried up in the summer.

Although the exact origin of Tahoka Lake's name is unclear, the last native inhabitants of the South Plains, the Comanche Indians, often visited the lake and may offer a clue about the name's origin. Baldwin Parker, son of Quanah Parker, recalled hearing elders speaking about the lake and its fresh, drinkable water, and Colonel Martin Crimmings, a cavalryman who was in the area in the 1870s, produced research detailing Great Plains place names that corroborated this. The Comanche word *tohoko* reportedly means "fresh water."

During the second half of the nineteenth century, a new phase of the lake's history began. The advent of the Red River War, more than one hundred miles to the north of the lake, saw an increased effort by the U.S. military to force Comanche Indians onto the reservation at Fort Sill. Although Tahoka Lake was not the site of any major actions of the campaigns, some minor skirmishes did occur at or around the lake.

Tahoka Lake in Lynn County. *Courtesy Austin Allison.*

In November 1874, the Fourth Cavalry under the command of Colonel Ranald Mackenzie came upon and attacked a small group of Comanche Indians several miles west of the lake. They camped at the lake on the night of November 4 and the next day skirmished with a small group of warriors at the lake. The next year, a column of Shafter's Tenth Cavalry passed by the lake. Eventually, this increased military presence in the area and the subsequent relocation of Comanche Indians to Fort Sill made settlement in the area possible.

Previously, as early as the 1850s, New Mexican sheepherders grazed and watered their flocks at Tahoka Lake, but permanent settlement around the lake and Lynn County did not occur until the late 1870s. In 1880, the national census recorded only eight residents living in Lynn County, and all at "Tehoca Lake."

Ed Ryan raised sheep, and a family of seven by the name of the McDonnell raised cattle on the banks of Tahoka Lake. Over the next twenty years, the population of the county nearly doubled, and the 1900 census showed that the county was still dominated by the livestock raisers.

In the 1890s, Christopher Columbus (C.C.) Slaughter came into possession of more than 140,000 acres of land surrounding the lake, between the Currycomb Ranch to the east and the T-Bar Ranch to the west. The ranch became known as the Tahoka Lake Ranch. From 1897 through 1907, Slaughter's foreman and manager, Jack Alley, had his headquarters at Tahoka Lake.

The topography surrounding the lake and year-round access to water made the site attractive to stock raisers. Like similar lakes in the county and region, Tahoka Lake had the capability to support, at least temporarily, large cattle operations. In one year alone, Slaughter's Tahoka Lake Ranch delivered 2,400 head of cattle.

The ranch, however, was short-lived. In 1902, a ruling by the Supreme Court of Texas severely limited Slaughter's ability to keep re-leasing the land from the State of Texas. Therefore, as his leases expired, he strategically informed his acquaintances that the land was going to be sold by the state. He hoped to hinder homesteaders by helping his friends move onto land he once controlled. By these means, Jack Alley acquired most of the ranch land surrounding the lake.

Tahoka Lake also lends its name to a flowering plant common on the southern Great Plains. *Machaeranthera tanacetifolia*, the Tahoka Daisy, or prairie aster, was first noticed blooming along the shores of the lake by Effie Alley, the wife of Jack Alley. A May 28, 1970 issue of the *Lynn County News* related that the lilac-petaled flower was first noticed at the lake around 1898 but received its name when Mrs. W.A. Myrick Sr. of Lubbock took the flower to Lubbock and dubbed the plant the Tahoka Daisy. You can read more about it later in this book, in Part VIII.

Today, conservation efforts exist to preserve the Tahoka Lake pasture and the history around the lake. Texas Tech University has conducted archaeological studies of specific sites around the lake, including remnants of sheepherder fences located near the lake. The land immediately surrounding the lake has never been plowed and still offers a unique look into native plant life in the region.

QUANAH PARKER

Paul H. Carlson

Quanah Parker, one of the more famous Native Americans of the Great Plains, spent a large portion of his life in Texas. The son of a Comanche warrior, Peta Nocona (or Puttack) and an Anglo woman, Cynthia Ann Parker (or Naduah, her Comanche name), he was born in about 1845. As a youth, his name was Quanah, and as an adult, when he quit his mobile hunting life to settle on the Comanche-Kiowa Reservation in 1875, he adopted his mother's family name, Parker.

Quanah's father was a warrior of some success, but he was not a chief. The army interpreter Horace Jones, who knew Peta Nocona well, said that Nocona "was not even a 'big man' among the Comanches." Yet he was a hunter-warrior of some distinction, for he needed to support three or four wives and their children.

Quanah's mother, kidnapped by Comanches in an 1836 raid at Parker's Fort near Groesbeck in Limestone County when she was nine years old, grew to womanhood among her captors. About five or six years after the kidnapping, she married Nocona. Like many Hispanic and Anglo female captives among the Comanches, she became a "chore wife" to a man who needed more than one wife to care for the family tipis, watch over children and especially tan animal hides and prepare bison robes for sale.

Quanah had a younger brother named Peanuts or Pecos, perhaps three or four years his junior, and a much younger baby sister named Topsannah (or Prairie Flower). He grew up among the Nokoni division of Comanches, and

Quanah Parker, circa 1890,
about age forty-five.

in his youth he played games, hunted small animals (birds and prairie dogs) and tended to his family's horse herd. As an adolescent, with his father's permission, he began going on raids to capture horses and gain honor.

In December 1860, Quanah and his entire family, with several others, may have been on a successful bison hunt along the Pease River. In any case, on the nineteenth, a few days after Quanah with his father and brother had left their little hunting camp along Mule Creek just upstream from the sand-filled river in present Foard County, a command of Texas Rangers, militiamen and federal soldiers attacked the hunting camp. They killed seven Comanches, captured Quanah's mother and baby sister and destroyed tons of bison products the Comanches had collected to get through the coming winter. Quanah was about fifteen years old.

Not long after their mother's capture, Quanah and his brother joined the Quahadi division, whose home territory included the Llano Estacado. Among the Quahadis, Quanah grew tall, erect and handsome. As an adult, like most Indians of the Plains, he was a superb horseman. He was also a charismatic leader and skilled hunter and warrior.

In October 1871, if our sources are correct, Quanah led a daring Comanche attack into and through the temporary military encampment of Colonel Ranald Mackenzie of the Fourth Cavalry, one of the federal army's most successful officers. Mackenzie's troops had been in pursuit of the Quahadis in West Texas. Their camp was near the mouth of Blanco Canyon, and in a late-night raid on October 10, Quanah led his men, yelling and shouting and making as much noise as possible, through the campsite. They scattered horses and ran off with many of them.

The next day, Quanah and his party gave chase to a company of Mackenzie's men looking to find the missing horses and the Indians who stole them. During the charge, Quanah killed one of the men whose horse had stumbled. He then led his Comanches out of the canyon and across the Llano Estacado.

Less than three years later, in the spring of 1874, Quanah was one of the Comanche-Cheyenne-Kiowa leaders in the famous fight at Adobe Walls in the Canadian River Valley. Upset with the way bison hunters were destroying bison, Quanah organized a multi-nation attack against the hunters. It did not go well for the Indians, and in 1875, the army responded in a major campaign against those living off their reservations. Many, including Quanah and his band, peacefully headed for the reservation.

On the reservation, Quanah adopted his mother's family name, rose to a position of prominence and became wealthy through investments and relationships with Texas cattlemen grazing cattle on Comanche lands. He became a friend of President Theodore Roosevelt, built a large twenty-one-room home, acquired seven wives and sired many children.

Federal authorities made him chief of the Comanches. He became a man of two worlds on the reservation. He accepted many Anglo ways, but he did not give up his polygamist household, he did not adopt Christianity, he encouraged the use of peyote and he wore his hair in long braids. When he died in 1911, he was buried in full Comanche regalia.

PART III

CORSET STAYS
TO CATTLE

By the time the Apache, Comanche and Kiowa tribes were being forced to surrender their beloved hunting grounds on the Llano Estacado, cattlemen from Texas and elsewhere were poised ready to claim the vast prairies of grass. One of these was the famous Charles Goodnight, who established the JA Ranch in Palo Duro Canyon in 1876. In this chapter, we learn another facet of Goodnight's legend—that of his invention of the chuck wagon.

This section also documents the role of two other lesser known ranchers: Cass O. Edwards of Fort Worth, who established the T-Bar Ranch in Lynn County, and Charles K. Warren of distant Three Oaks, Michigan, who founded the Muleshoe Ranch in Bailey County. These cowmen were typical of the dozens who invested in the region, but none matched the skill and fortitude of Amarillo's Mathew "Bones" Hooks, who overcame years of prejudice to become one of its leading citizens.

The story of the development of the National Ranching Heritage Center at Texas Tech University, which opened in 1976, concludes this chapter.

THE T-BAR RANCH IN LYNN COUNTY

Don Abbe

I n the years after the Civil War, demand for beef led to the rapid expansion of the western ranching industry. As the Native Americans who occupied the land were forced onto reservations, the ranching frontier swept across West Texas and the Llano Estacado.

The Panhandle-Plains region of Texas was typical in the growth of the ranch industry. As the Comanches and Kiowas were forced onto reservations in Indian Territory, stockmen moved into the region. First, in the mid-1870s, the sheep raising *pastores* came from both central Texas and New Mexico. Soon, these groups were supplanted by the cattle rancher.

Adjacent to and across the southern Llano Estacado, ranching enterprises popped up. Between 1873 and the mid-1880s, virtually the entire region was occupied by ranches. Almost all of these ventures were founded, and funded, by investors from far away. Some were from North Texas or Central Texas. Others were from the northern and eastern United States, while others still were financed by foreign companies.

One such venture was the T-Bar Ranch in Lynn County, established by Cass O. Edwards and his brother George. Cass Edwards was a successful rancher in Tarrant County when he decided to join the rush to the West. He ranched first, in Crosby County in 1879, but moved in 1882, when he established the T-Bar Ranch in west-central Lynn County. He headquartered his new ranch on the north side of the Double Lakes.

Cowboys move cattle during a roundup on the T-Bar Ranch in Lynn County, around the 1930s. *Photo from Frank Reeves Collection, Southwest Collection, Texas Tech University.*

Since Edwards was already a successful rancher, the success of the T-Bar was virtually guaranteed. Following a time-honored business model in the Texas ranching business, Edwards began to both purchase land and lease land from the state. He purchased railroad land at inexpensive rates whenever the opportunity arose. He also paid his cowboys to file on up to four sections of school land at a time, as Texas law allowed. Edwards then purchased the land from the cowboys after they had "proved up" the claim. In some ways, he was ahead of the times, as he realized that the ownership of the land was a far better business strategy than leasing.

Likewise, as many businessmen prefer to do, Edwards shared the risks and rewards with several others. Cass Edwards, W.C. Young, Jasper Hayes and L.S. Gholson—all experienced cattlemen—formed the Tahoka Cattle Company, with a capitalization of $200,000. Created in November 1883, the new company financed the move to Lynn County and the establishment of the ranch.

The collapse of the western ranching industry in 1885 and 1886 hurt the ranch, but it forged ahead nevertheless. By the end of the 1880s, the T-Bar contained about 100 sections of land, or about 70,000 acres. In the 1890s, the ranch enlarged by continuing its strategy of buying land during a time when political pressure by farmers was ending the leasing of land by ranches. By the 1900s, the ranch held about 87,000 acres, or 136 sections.

Edwards's drive to actually own ranchland, and not lease it, saved the T-Bar. In 1902, in a major Texas land case, *Ketner v. Rogan*, the farmers won a significant legal victory. The Texas Supreme Court ruled that leased school lands must be offered for sale before another lease could be signed. This doomed many of the great ranches of the South Plains and Panhandle.

After 1902, as leases expired, small land rushes took place in many area counties. In Lynn County, the T-Bar suffered only limited damage because of its limited amount of leased land. Between 1902 and 1910, the ranch lost about seventeen thousand acres to newly arriving farmers, most of it in the south-central part of the county.

The T-Bar Ranch was historically divided into three working divisions: the Three Lakes, the Double Lakes and the Guthrie Lake Divisions. All were fenced and held either Hereford or mixed-breed shorthorn cattle. As the ranch entered the 1930s, it was a stable operation, adequately funded and profitable in most years.

However, changes took place in the ownership structure over the years. In 1909, Cass Edwards's wife, Sally, passed away, and in 1916, he married Mollie Childers of Benbrook. As a result, the long-term ownership of the ranch was altered. Cass dissolved the Tahoka Cattle Company and became its sole owner. He then divided the ranch into three parts, and upon his death one third went to his son, Crawford Edwards; one third to his grandson (Crawford's son) Cass Edwards II; and the other third to his second wife.

This restructuring did not occur until the early 1940s, when Crawford Edwards died in 1941 and Cass O. Edwards in 1942. This left two-thirds of the ranch in the hands of Cass Edwards II. Over the years, the heirs of Cass and Crawford regained some of the land inherited by Mollie. Today, after more than 135 years, the T-Bar remains a viable and active ranching enterprise.

FROM CORSET STAYS TO CATTLE

THE BEGINNING OF THE MULESHOE RANCH

David J. Murrah

While most historic cattle ranches on the Llano Estacado were established by Texas cattlemen, one of the most iconic—the Muleshoe Ranch—was created by the son of a Michigan manufacturer of women's corset stays made from turkey feather quills.

Charles K. Warren was born in the southern Michigan village of Three Oaks in 1870. At sixteen, after a summer trip to his uncle's farm in Missouri, he fell in love with the West and longed to return. In 1890, young Charlie quit school and became a traveling salesman for his father's Featherbone Company, selling whips and corset stays, an invention that made his father wealthy. But he longed to be a cowboy, and in late 1890, he turned in his samples and headed for Texas.

He first landed in Dallas and there hired out to work as a cowboy on the Square and Compass Ranch near present-day Post, beginning work on January 1, 1891. The other cowboys quickly nicknamed Warren "the Colonel" because he arrived on the ranch dressed in a suit, white shirt, derby hat and patent leather shoes.

Charlie wrote descriptive letters to his parents back in Michigan, trying to allay their fears about his life on the frontier. "I have been out here since Jan. 1st and have not had a chance to spend a cent," he wrote after three weeks on the job. "Cards and whiskey are forbidden on the ranch so you can see as long as a man stays away from town, he is far from many temptations."

Charles Warren's father, E.K. Warren, invented Featherbone, made from turkey feather quills, as a replacement for whalebone in corset stays and buggy whips. This ad appeared in about 1890.

And he added, "It is only 70 miles to town [Colorado City]. I shall be careful in habits, etc., and not go to town with the boys, so please don't worry."

A few months later, he vividly described his experience in a night stampede:

> *We had three thousand two-year old steers and drove them to the bedding ground, watered them, and about sunset, they began to lay down and chew their cuds....It was dark, no wind, warm and cloudy....I could hear the boys humming a song as they rode round and round, their large Mexican spurs gingle [sic] as they rode round and round. I fell to sleep.*
>
> *About 11 pm, it commenced to lightning and then to rain in torrents and the cattle began to drift before the storm. The boss could be heard yelling, "Saddle up, all! Saddle up all!" The cattle broke at 2 am and by that time the storm was terrible. We could see nothing, only as the lightning flashed, only the bellow of frantic cattle and the roar of thunder could be heard and*

so I rode on as hard as I could go til toward morning when the rain ceased and when it was light enough to see.

I found I had followed about 700 steers…and was over 20 miles from camp. I rounded them up and kept them grazing til about 4 yesterday evening when 4 of the boys came to help me drive them in.

And, Charlie nonchalantly concluded, "Such is the life of a Cowboy on a rainy night and yet there is something fascinating about it all."

Young Warren was indeed fascinated with West Texas, especially with the so-called code of the West. "Two cattlemen rode onto a yearling yesterday south of here 12 miles," he wrote to his father in February 1891. "Both claimed it. One said if he was not to have it, no man could and shot the calf whereupon the other man pulled his six-shooter and shot the first man 3 times and killed him. One of our boys was at the inquest—verdict, self defense."

During his stay on the Square and Compass, young Warren wrote several letters to his father asking for financial aid to invest in Texas cattle, horses or land. Instead, his father, E.K. Warren, persuaded his son to return to Michigan to manage the family farm. He also became more involved in the Featherbone Company and became its vice-president.

But Charlie never forgot his Texas adventure and planned to return and buy his own ranch. That dream began to take shape when the vast XIT Ranch began selling large tracts of its 3 million acres, which spread from present-day Levelland northward to the top of the Texas Panhandle.

In 1903, Charlie Warren and his father paid $100,000 for the forty-thousand-acre YL Ranch, which stretched across northern Bailey County, which at one time been a part of the vast XIT Ranch. The venture soon became known as the Muleshoe Ranch and eventually led to the establishment of the town named Muleshoe.

FROM CORSET STAYS TO CATTLE

THE LATER YEARS OF THE MULESHOE RANCH

David J. Murrah

I n 1903, Charles Warren and his father, E.K. Warren of Three Oaks, Michigan, purchased the forty-thousand-acre YL Ranch, which covered the northern end of Bailey County, once a part of the famed 3-million-acre XIT Ranch. The ranch included the present site of Muleshoe, Texas, which they helped to establish in 1913.

The origin of the name, Muleshoe, which eventually became the name of the Warren ranch as well as a town and even a national wildlife refuge, is shrouded in folklore. Initially, the Warrens referred to their new Texas venture as the YL, but in 1907, they purchased from Kansas City cattlemen W.D. and F.W. Johnson an adjacent ranch on which the Johnsons may have used the muleshoe brand. Later, when the Johnsons acquired the Magnolia Ranch in Borden County, they used a muleshoe brand there on a ranch that is still in existence and widely known as the Muleshoe.

The Warren purchase of the Johnson Ranch in Bailey and adjoining counties more than doubled their holdings, and through subsequent leases and purchases, their ranch grew to more than 150,000 acres, covering all of northern Bailey County and southern Parmer County. Then, in 1909, Charlie Warren acquired a ranch in Mexico whose cattle bore the U Bar (U-) brand. Subsequently, he applied that brand to all his herds.

In all likelihood, the resemblance of the brand used by the Johnsons and Warren's U Bar were close enough to apply the commonality of a muleshoe

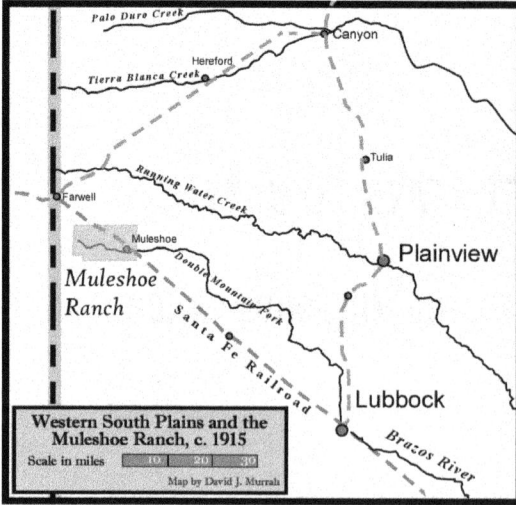

The Muleshoe Ranch was located primarily in Bailey County. *Map by David J. Murrah.*

to be the name of the enlarged Texas ranch. By 1913, when the Santa Fe built its so-called Coleman cut-off from Coleman to Farwell to connect with its main line, Warren allowed the railroad to designate the new town being built at the site of the ranch's loading pens as Muleshoe.

The arrival of the railroad spurred rising land values, and with the outbreak of World War I, high cotton prices stimulated a renewed demand for farmland. As a result, Warren began selling land to farmers, and Bailey County grew rapidly, with its population increasing from five hundred to more than five thousand in the 1920s, and the Michigan entrepreneur reaped a nice profit.

But not all Warren investments worked out as smoothly as it did in Texas. When revolution broke out in Mexico in 1910, Warren soon found himself caught between warring sides, and he had to pay bribes to both the government and revolutionaries, including Pancho Villa. The Warren foreman in Mexico, Bunk Spencer, was captured and held for ransom six times before being murdered.

However, because cattle could be produced in Mexico at half the cost of American cattle, Warren rode out the revolution and made the ranch profitable in spite of the thievery and bribery. As a result, the Warren ranch and farm empire eventually grew to include more than 500,000 acres and twenty-five thousand cattle on its three ranches at Muleshoe, in southern New Mexico and in Mexico.

E.K. Warren, the inventor of Featherbone (and whose money paid for his son's ranching ventures), died in 1919. Then, in 1932, Charles Warren died at age sixty-one, leaving the vast operation in the hands of the family corporation, headed by his son E.K. Warren and brother-in-law George Lackey.

In the 1940s, the Warren family continued to expand its holdings by acquiring additional ranches in New Mexico and Colorado but lost their Mexican ranches shortly after World War II when Mexican politicians forced them to sell to them at one-third of the original purchase price.

By the early 1950s, the elder members of the Warren family no longer retained controlling interest in the company, and the new investors apparently had no taste for ranching. In 1954, they sold all the remaining ranches, including the Muleshoe. About the same time, Warren's Featherbone Company—which had shifted from making corset stays to manufacturing ribbon, elastic and braid—closed its Michigan factory in 1956 and moved to Gainesville, Georgia, where it made baby clothes until 2005.

Today, in Three Oaks, Michigan, there are a number of memorials, including a statue of Featherbone founder E.K. Warren. And in Georgia in 2005, the Featherbone factory there became a memorial by being converted to a "communiversity" by Gus Whalen Jr., a great-grandson of E.K. Warren. Through Warren Featherbone Foundation, the old Featherbone factory provides continuing education for North Georgia residents.

But perhaps the best memorial to the family is the iconic Texas town of Muleshoe, which proudly bears the name of the Warren Muleshoe Ranch.

CHUCK WAGONS

Monica Hightower

One of the icons of American ranching is the chuck wagon, which was used by virtually every ranch until the development of pickup trucks and trailers. Its origin is linked to one of the Llano Estacado's earliest ranchers.

Charles Goodnight was an American cattle rancher often known as the "Father of the Texas Panhandle." Following the Civil War, Goodnight began herding Texas Longhorn cattle from West Texas to supply the army in New Mexico or miners in Colorado. In 1866, Goodnight and his partner, Oliver Loving, drove one of the first herds of cattle along what would become known as the Goodnight-Loving Trail. The trail eventually carried Texas cattle all the way to Wyoming.

Out of the necessity to feed the cowboys on this long trail drive, Charles Goodnight is credited with inventing the chuck wagon. He began with the purchase of a used government wagon and had it completely rebuilt in seasoned bois d'arc, the toughest wood available and fitted with iron axles to make sure it could handle the rigors of the trail drive.

The distinguishing feature of the chuck wagon was the sloping box on the rear with a hinged lid that lowered to become a cook's work table. The box was the width of the wagon and had shelves and drawers for holding food and cooking or food preparation utensils. Cowboys of the time called food "chuck," so the box was called a chuck box and the wagon became known as a chuck wagon.

Goodnight's chuck wagon was copied widely and changed little in the years that followed. Most of the later ones had the same basic design but varied according to what the builder had available. Generally they were large, sturdy, four-wheeled wagons with bows across the top covered with a canvas sheet.

A cowhide stretched beneath the wagon bed was used to carry wood or cow chips for cooking fuel on the trail. In the front of the wagon was a jockey box, used for storing tools possibly needed on the trail.

On the trail drive, the chuck wagon became the headquarters. It was a place for cowboys to eat their meals, their social and recreational spot for sharing the events of the day and, if there happened to be a musician in the group, their entertainment venue as well.

The chuck wagon cook was in charge of the wagon and food preparation. He was the absolute authority, and he was largely unquestioned. Even the wagon boss walked softly in the vicinity of the chuck wagon cook. Wagon cooks in general had the reputation of being ill-tempered, but it's no wonder, as their working conditions were difficult and their hours were long.

The cook's job required that he get up earlier than the cowboys to prepare the breakfast. And when the herd was moving, he had to drive ahead of the herd scouting for the next camp spot and have a hot meal ready when the cowboys arrived. Trail conditions often left the cook short of fuel or water. He was constantly experiencing the elements of wind, rain, sand, mud, insects and rattlesnakes while preparing meals. In addition, the cook also served as a barber, doctor, banker and mediator if a disturbance arose.

A typical day's food on the trail was hot bread, dried fruit, coffee, beans, potatoes, gravy and maybe meat. If the cook had time and was so inclined, he would make a dessert as a special treat for the cowboys. Usually it was a two-crust pie made with apples or some other dried fruit. To let the steam out, he often cut the outfit's brand into the top crust of the pie.

The atmosphere and language around a chuck wagon was likely colorful considering the hard work and hard conditions. There were, however, definite rules of behavior around the chuck wagon. Most were unwritten laws understood by the cowhands. Here are just a few:

- Riders approaching the campsite stayed downwind from the chuck wagon to prevent dust from blowing into the food or preparation area.
- No horse should be tied to the chuck wagon wheel or hobbled too close to camp.
- Cowboys never crowded around the cook fire.

The historic HX chuck wagon, owned by Ferris and Monica Hightower, is set up and ready to start cooking. *Courtesy Monica Hightower.*

- No scuffling around the chuck wagon while meals were being prepared.
- No cowboy helped himself to food without Cookie's permission.
- Cowboys never used the cook's worktable as a dining table; they sat on the ground and used their laps instead.
- A cowboy never took the last piece of anything unless he was sure the rest of the group was finished eating.
- If a man got up during a meal to refill his cup with coffee and someone yelled, "Man at the pot," he was expected to fill all the cups held out to him as well as his own.
- No food was to be left on your plate.
- After a meal, the cowboys always scraped their plates clean and put them in the "wreck pan" for washing.

Long cattle drives disappeared generally by the late 1890s, but chuck wagons can still be found today on ranches, at historical and educational events and at chuck wagon cooking competitions. Today, a unique part of our American history is preserved by a relatively small group of avid chuck wagon enthusiasts.

MATHEW "BONES" HOOKS

PIONEER, COWBOY, CIVIC LEADER

Marty Kuhlman

Mathew "Bones" Hooks was an important figure in the ranching and civic development of the Llano Estacado.

Born in Robertson County, Texas, in 1867 to former slaves Alex and Annie Hooks, Mathew received the nickname of "Bones" due to his small build as a child. He started his first job, driving a meat wagon for a butcher, at the age of seven. The next year, he participated in a cattle drive as he drove a wagon to Colorado for Steve Donald. He continued to work for Donald and soon became a respected horse wrangler.

Hooks worked on various ranches and took part in many cattle drives. In 1886, he moved to Texarkana in East Texas to start a grocery store. Fortunately, for future West Texas, he returned west after eighteen months because of a warning posted on his store door to "get out" signed by a white supremacist group.

He lived in Clarendon for twenty-three years and became involved in establishing the first African American church in West Texas, St. Stephens Baptist Church. He also went to Fort Worth to find a preacher for the church and to preside over his own marriage to Miss Anna Crenshaw in Clarendon.

Hooks became known as a top horse wrangler and worked on a number of West Texas ranches, including the XIT. He broke horses for Charles Goodnight and recalled that Goodnight had no problem hiring Black cowboys. Of course, Hooks did face discrimination, especially in towns like Mobeetie and Memphis.

Hooks worked with another cowboy, Tom Clayton, in training horses and selling them around the Panhandle. After Clayton died when a horse fell on him, Anna suggested that they move to Amarillo so Hooks could find a safer line of work. In 1900, he became a porter and Anna a maid at the Hotel Elmhurst. Hooks later took a job as a porter on the Santa Fe Railroad in 1909.

On one train trip in the Panhandle, Hooks overheard four men talking about a horse that could not be broken. Hooks told the men he could ride the horse. The men scoffed but took Hooks's wager of twenty-five dollars.

When the train stopped in Pampa, where the "unrideable" black mustang "Old Bob" waited,

Mathew "Bones" Hooks.
Courtesy Amarillo.com.

Hooks booted and spurred and removed the white porter's jacket. Getting off the train, he "combed that bronc from his ears to his tail, rode him to a standstill, collected his money, and was back on the train when it pulled out seven minutes later."

He and his wife made a home in Amarillo (Anna died in 1920). Hooks was the second African American to live in Amarillo. Since Whites balked at having Black residents live near them, Hooks established a separate Black-only community in Amarillo. Hooks convinced Mayor Lee Bivins to provide financial support to open North Heights. Hooks invested time and money to establish a drugstore/general store in the community.

He had a strong interest in helping young people, and even though he had no children of his own, he became a father figure. Since Black citizens could not join Amarillo's youth organization, the Maverick Club, Hooks started the Dogie Club in 1932 and served as a mentor to many young African American boys. He led the Dogie Club in activities such as camping, planting trees and sports and held discussions on life, good citizenship and the whys of discrimination. He told the boys that soon segregation would end and they'd be able to swim in the city pool.

Former member Charles Kemp stated that Hooks "made you feel like you were somebody." "It was the biggest thing that ever happened to me," Eddie Moore agreed. "If it hadn't been for the Dogie Club a lot of us would have gone astray."

Hooks is probably best known for bringing white flowers to the funerals of Panhandle pioneers. He also sent a single white flower to living dignitaries,

including Franklin Roosevelt, Will Rogers and Sir Winston Churchill. In his lifetime, he sent out more than five hundred white flowers to people.

Hooks broke racial barriers on a number of occasions, such as being the first African American to sit on a Potter County grand jury and the first Black member of the XIT Association, as well as other groups.

An example of the respect that Hooks had in the community was that the newspaper, the *Amarillo Globe-Times*, started a fund for him when he became ill and hired a housekeeper to care for him.

In 1951, Hooks died, and his funeral at the Mount Zion Baptist Church was crowded with diverse mourners. Each person respectfully placed a single white flower on his coffin.

Mathew Hooks was later inducted into the National Cowboys of Color Museum and Hall of Fame in Fort Worth.

THE NATIONAL RANCHING HERITAGE CENTER OF TEXAS TECH UNIVERSITY

A BRIEF HISTORY

Scott White

With the Llano Estacado's great ranching heritage, it was only a matter of time before someone would envision a museum to help preserve its story.

In 1966, Dr. Grover E. Murray, then president of Texas Technological College, enlisted Dr. William Curry Holden to create a multicultural museum complex about arid and semi-arid lands. The plan included the creation of a living history ranching museum. That same year, a group of area ranchers, businessmen and professional historians met at the Pioneer Hotel in downtown Lubbock to develop a support organization for this new museum.

The group organized the Ranch Headquarters Association (RHA) and began to acquire several historic ranch structures for the college. The Ranch Headquarters was designed to be part of a seventy-six-acre area, which would be the Texas Tech Museum Complex on the Texas Tech campus. It was to be located between an outdoor horticultural exhibit on twenty acres that featured dry land plants along with arid land ethnic exhibits. On the other side of the RHA, on thirteen acres, would be an exhibit of windmills of the world.

The RHA involvement quickly enlarged the planning for the museum into an historical park called the Ranch Headquarters, which would showcase the growth of ranching. The RHA worked for more than a year, choosing buildings to authentically tell the story of the heritage of ranching.

With other ranchers and ranching families, the RHA acquired donations for reconstruction and restoration work.

The structures for the Ranch Headquarters were chosen to represent the birth, growth and maturity of ranching in the region west of the Mississippi, just as Mount Vernon and Colonial Williamsburg represent the nation's history east of the river.

By September 1969, seventeen buildings located throughout Texas had been selected for the new museum. All the structures (houses, corrals, barns and windmills) were then relocated to the Ranch Headquarters from their original locations so they could be restored and furnished to their proper historical period. Some of the buildings were moved intact, while a number were dismantled, moved and rebuilt.

During August 1970, the blacksmith shop from the Renderbrook-Spade Ranch became the first structure at the newly created Ranch Headquarters outdoor museum on the grounds of Texas Tech. This little red box and strip building arrived with all the equipment that had been housed in it for almost one hundred years.

This event convinced the Texas legislature that the project was supported by the ranching and university communities; it then appropriated funding for further preparation of the site. Texas governor Preston Smith proclaimed October 7, 1972, as Ranch Day in recognition of the efforts made by the Ranch Headquarters to preserve the ranching heritage and its visual symbols.

By 1974, nineteen buildings and three windmills comprised the site, although some structures needed restoration work. In 1975, the museum changed its name to the Ranching Heritage Center. An official opening date was set for 1976 to coincide with the national bicentennial celebration.

Before many historic buildings could be moved to the Ranch Headquarters, it was necessary to create a landscape of pathways and prepare locations, involving a great deal of earth work. The construction of barrier berms would require about forty-two thousand cubic yards of fill and topsoil. After the tornado of May 1970 ripped through Lubbock, its destruction provided an alternate source of construction material, and the RHC arranged with the City of Lubbock to deposit debris from the storm as foundation fill for the berms.

Material such as the remains of the old Pontiac house on Avenue Q was pushed into one mound, while roof tile from the Broadway Church of Christ created another. Texas Tech also provided caliche and excess dirt that had been stored on campus. Then, Company B, 980th Engineering Battalion,

The 1909 Barton House is the dominant feature of the forty-two outdoor structures at the National Ranching Heritage Center. *Courtesy National Ranching Heritage Center, Texas Tech University.*

U.S. Army Reserve, moved the dirt into place and shaped the berms during its training weekends.

On Friday, July 2, 1976, Lady Bird Johnson, wife of the former president of the United States, spoke at the dedication of the renamed and newly opened Ranching Heritage Center and the just-constructed DeVitt-Mallet orientation building during a typical West Texas dust and rain storm. Her speech followed the arrival of a longhorn cattle trail and truck drive, which began a week earlier in San Antonio passing through Kerrville, San Angelo, Stamford, Midland and ending in Lubbock.

The consul-generals of England, France, Germany, Spain and the ambassador of Mexico, as well as a number of local and state politicians, took part in the opening ceremonies, which lasted until Sunday night, July 4. Film and television star Dale Robertson acted as the master of ceremonies. More than 750 volunteers helped out on that weekend.

During the three days following opening activities, nearly twenty-five thousand visitors toured the Ranching Heritage Center, and for the month of July 1976, more than thirty thousand visitors from forty-seven states as well as the Canal Zone, Australia, Brazil, Canada, England, France, India,

Japan, Korea, Mexico, the Netherlands, South Africa, Spain, Sweden and West Germany passed through the center.

What began as the Ranch Headquarters museum now has more than forty historic structures, with a large and spacious interpretation center, and it is now known as the National Ranching Heritage Center, one of the nation's premier outdoor museums.

PART IV

THE LLANO ESTACADO

A PLACE OF REFUGE

The search for religious freedom runs deep in American history. The Pilgrims, Puritans, Roman Catholics, Baptists and other groups fled England and Europe to the frontier of the New World to find a way to worship as they pleased. More than two centuries later, the isolated Llano Estacado frontier offered a similar freedom to religious groups, including Quakers, German Catholics and Mennonites.

A Quaker, Paris Cox, brought the first permanent settlement to the Llano in 1878. Later came German Catholics, then Mennonites, and both groups have had a profound impact on the face of West Texas.

Some of this story has been recorded in more than 170 historical books and pamphlets written by a little-known Catholic priest, known by his pen name, F. Stanley, who took refuge and pastored churches for more than thirty years on his beloved Llano Estacado.

THE BUCKLE OF THE BIBLE BELT

RELIGION ON THE LLANO BEFORE 1930

David J. Murrah

The Llano Estacado is certainly a part of the label that describes West Texas as the "buckle of the Bible Belt" because of its historic ties to Protestant evangelical denominations. Before 1930, however, the region's isolation and land availability also served to attract enclaves of Catholics, Quakers, Mennonites and others.

By the 1850s, as Anglo cattlemen and farmers began to make incursions along the eastern approaches to West Texas, established Protestant groups—Methodist, Baptist and Presbyterian—were in the forefront of promoting religion. These groups had all secured footholds in Texas by 1836 and, by 1850, accounted for three-fourths of all established churches in the state.

By 1860, the Methodist Episcopal Church, South, was the largest denomination in the state. After the Civil War, it created in 1866 the Northwest Texas Conference, which along with its sister, the West Texas Conference, embraced three-fourths of the state; nonetheless, most of the region was still unsettled. Methodists used circuit riders to comb the frontier counties.

Baptists also devised an effective ministry through cooperating churches combined as associations to send missionaries to the frontier. By the end of the Reconstruction era in 1875, Baptists had become the largest denomination in the state.

However, on the Llano Estacado, two other groups pioneered the initial two churches there. The first was a colony representing the northern-based

Methodist Episcopal Church, established by Reverend Lewis Henry Carhart of Sherman, Texas. In 1878, he purchased 343 sections and founded the town of Clarendon. He promoted the colony widely and soon attracted settlers from many northern and eastern states, including seven retired Methodist ministers. By 1880, the pioneers had built a small church, for which Reverend Carhart purchased a large cast bell to call the faithful to worship. It was the first house of worship in the Panhandle.

Meanwhile, as you will learn in the following essay, Paris Cox of Indiana in 1879 led a group of Quakers to Lubbock County and built there in 1884 the first house of worship on the Llano Estacado proper.

Presbyterian missionaries also followed the frontier, and by the time the Texas & Pacific (T&P) railroad reached Abilene in 1881, Presbyterians were on hand to organize the city's first church. In 1885, Reverend C.W. Alexander came to Mobeetie to start Presbyterian work (see Jean Stuntz's essay, "Mary Jane Alexander: The First Woman Rancher in the Panhandle" in Part IV).

Once the railroads pushed across West Texas, the region began to grow. Baptists and Methodists competed to see who would be first in a community, but evangelization was usually marked by a spirit of cooperation, especially among these denominations. Generally, the first denomination to construct a building would share it with other congregations, and nearly all groups shared a union Sunday school.

Summer camp meetings also helped grow evangelical churches. The first camp meeting in the Llano Estacado area was probably one held in Blanco Canyon in 1886 in Floyd County, very near the site of the present Floydada Baptist Assembly grounds. When electricity came to rural areas in the 1920s and '30s, the summer camp meeting began to fade in favor of denominationally based revivals, which became the norm as the region became more urban and churches became larger. By the 1890s, all the Protestant denominations had adopted the practice of semiannual or annual revival meetings, which usually lasted from a week to two weeks.

Christian (Disciples of Christ) churches were established closely on the heels of Baptists and Methodists. By the 1890s, the Christian Church was sending preachers to Lubbock and Amarillo. The first Church of Christ on the Llano Estacado was established at Lockney in 1894. By 1910, others had been started at Claude, Hereford, Lubbock, Amarillo, McLean, Plainview, Tulia and the town of Panhandle.

The first Episcopal church in the Panhandle was established at Clarendon in 1889. Others soon followed at Amarillo, Plainview, Canyon, Midland and

The historic bell from the first church on the Llano Estacado at Clarendon now hangs at the Lakeview United Methodist Church in Dalhart. *Courtesy David J. Murrah.*

Lubbock. Slow growth kept the area a part of a missionary district until 1959, when the Diocese of Northwest Texas was created and subsequently seated in Lubbock.

In 1910, German Lutheran farmers from Indiana founded a church at Rhea in Parmer County in 1910. In 1911, another group of German Americans established a Lutheran church at Providence, northwest of Lockney, in Floyd County.

Catholics built a church at Clarendon in 1889. At Amarillo, the first Mass was probably celebrated in 1887 or 1888, but a church was not begun until 1903, two years after the establishment of St. Anthony's Hospital by the Sisters of the Incarnate Word. After 1900, German Catholic farmers, encouraged by land promoters, began migrating to the region from the Midwest. At Nazareth, in Castro County, Mass was celebrated by new arrivals in 1903, and the new community grew rapidly. Soon, other immigration led to strong German enclaves and Catholic work at Umbarger, Happy, Olton, Pep, Slaton, Littlefield, Perico, Vega, White Deer and Germania.

The Mexican Revolution that began in 1910 also spurred Catholic growth in West Texas among Hispanics. Due to persecution in Mexico, thousands of Catholics fled to the United States, prompting the creation of the Diocese of Amarillo in 1927.

In 1906, Mennonites began immigrating to West Texas when a group from the Midwest purchased land in eastern Hale County near Plainview under the leadership of Mennonite minister Peter B. Snyder. There, they built a schoolhouse, which also served as their church, and by 1909 they had a congregation of nearly fifty. The community survived the disastrous drought of 1917–18 but could not sustain through the poor years of the 1920s. In 1925, the church was disbanded, as most of the community returned to the Midwest or joined other congregations.

Meanwhile, two other groups of Mennonites purchased land in 1914 near Littlefield in Lamb County. However, the severe drought that began in 1917 on the plains, and the threat of conscription into the U.S. Army, soon decimated the new colonies. Since then, a large colony has settled on the Llano Estacado, and that story is related in the last three essays in this chapter.

PARIS COX AND THE QUAKERS

Jack Becker

The names of most of the major streets in Lubbock are obvious: University goes by Texas Tech, Slide Road goes to Slide and Clovis Highway goes to Clovis, New Mexico…but Quaker Avenue? Quaker Avenue is named for the first group of permanent Anglo-American settlers on the South Plains—a small group of Quakers led by Paris Cox, who established the first permanent agricultural settlement on the South Plains in the fall of 1878. Cox named the little village Marietta after his wife.

Cox first saw the future site of Marietta in the early 1870s while hunting buffalo as a hide hunter. From a small rise of land west of Henry C. "Hank" Smith's ranch in Blanco Canyon, Cox reportedly said, "Here by the will of God will be my home." It took, however, more than five years for Cox to make his wish a reality.

Born on October 17, 1846, near Asheboro, North Carolina, into a family of devout Quakers, Cox, like many others of that faith, had strong pacifist and abolitionist beliefs. At the beginning of the Civil War, Cox was nearly fifteen and had to flee to Westfield, Indiana, to avoid conscription into the Confederate army. While in Indiana, he married Mary C. Ferguson, a schoolteacher. Later, with his father-in-law's backing, he opened a sawmill, which prospered for a time.

After the war, in 1876, he returned to Texas to purchase the land he had promised himself to own. He also secured the right to resell the land to others for fifty cents per acre. After securing a deed to the land, Cox returned to Indiana and began organizing his return to the Llano Estacado.

He recruited several other Quaker families to join him, sold his sawmill and began his journey west, which led to the establishment of the first permanent community in Lubbock County. Almost immediately, the little community began to play an important role in the early history of Lubbock and Crosby Counties.

Cox was a very well-organized man. Before moving to his new home, he contracted with Hank Smith, an early pioneer, to dig a well for the new community, plow up thirty acres of prairie and plant it in a variety of crops for the new settlers. Smith reported that he found useable water at sixty-five feet.

The small group of Quakers moved on to the South Plains in the fall of 1878 and included Cox, his wife and their two sons, along with three other families. Unfortunately, their timing could not have been worse, as the winter of 1878–79 was a severe one.

Only Cox and his family had the foresight to build a sod house, while the other families lived in tents. In the spring of 1879, when the weather allowed, the three other families moved back to Indiana, leaving the Cox family alone on the South Plains.

But Cox and his family remained, worked hard and promoted the area to other Quakers. In the years that followed, the community grew as Quakers from Indiana and North Carolina joined them. Their crops did well, and the weather moderated. By 1882, due to Cox's hard work and foresight, ten families were calling Marietta home.

By 1884, the little town had grown to the point that it could support a post office, but since there was already a Marietta, Texas, the town changed its name in honor of its location, Estacado. In 1886, Estacado became the county seat of Crosby County (even though the community was actually in Lubbock County), and Cox became the county's first district court clerk.

Cox did not live long enough to see the town he worked so hard to build prosper. After battling throat cancer, he died on November 2, 1888, at only forty-two years of age and is buried at the cemetery southwest of town. Just two years after his death, Estacado boasted of a population of two hundred, with a school, church, a general store and a newspaper.

Unfortunately, Estacado went into a decline in the early 1890s due to drought and the discovery by surveyors that Estacado was, in fact, in Lubbock, not Crosby County. In a hotly contested election, the citizens of Crosby County voted to move the seat of county government to Emma, a

The Quaker congregation at Estacado, circa 1885. *Courtesy Southwest Collection, Texas Tech University.*

town more centrally located within Crosby County. After the seat of county government moved and following several failed crop years, Estacado went into a rapid decline.

Today, little remains of the once prosperous Quaker community that Paris Cox worked so hard to establish. But his memory lives on in a street commemorating the small but determined religious community, the first permanent settlement on the South Plains.

F. STANLEY

THE PRIEST WHO BECAME A HISTORIAN OF THE LLANO ESTACADO

Christena Stephens

While doing research at the Holy Family Church in Nazareth, Texas, someone told me about one of its former priests who was born on Halloween. His personality was always described to me as generous and jovial. However, it was a locked bookcase at the church rectory that captured my unwavering attention about this joyful priest. There, behind its wooden doors, I found most of the books and booklets the priest wrote, along with his handwritten notes. To match the priest's disposition, every book was bound in yellow sunflower covers.

Long before John Wayne and Clint Eastwood glamorized cowboy movies, this young boy from Greenwich, New York, became enamored of everything the Old West offered. Although he became a priest, he also wrote more than 170 books and pamphlets on Texas and New Mexico history.

Born as Francis Louis Crocchiola on Halloween in 1908, this little boy would eventually be known simply as Father Stanley, or by his pen name, F. Stanley. At age thirty, he was ordained into the Franciscan Order of Atonement in Washington, D.C. Nine years later, he contracted tuberculosis, which made his East Coast ministry challenging.

While health ailments can be detrimental to most people, being diagnosed with tuberculosis became a blessing for Father Stanley. The order gave him the opportunity to move to the semi-arid Llano Estacado in 1939, to a pastorate of his own choosing. He picked Hereford, where he hoped the dry climate would aid in his recovery.

He received a rude introduction to High Plains of West Texas, for when he arrived in Hereford by train in February 1939, black dust was blowing so hard that he could not even make out any of the surrounding landscape or town—it must have been harrowing for him. When the dust cleared, he saw the outstretched expanse of Hereford, home to 2,500 souls. But he was finally in his beloved adopted West.

A few years later, he was sent to Taos, New Mexico, and served at churches or missions in Raton, Villanueva, Sapello and Pecos. There, he gained an appreciation for the rich religious and secular history of the region, and while in Raton, he started spending every spare minute researching and writing. His first published book was entitled *Raton Chronicle*, published in 1948; it became the first of many, written under his pen name.

While serving in New Mexico, Stanley wrote pamphlet histories on practically every village in northeastern New Mexico. His work caught the attention of Bishop Laurence Fitzsimons of the Amarillo Diocese, who also had a passion for history. As a result, in January 1952 Stanley moved to Amarillo to become the Amarillo diocesan historian and continued his historical research in earnest.

Father Stanley stands before a Pueblo Mission in northern New Mexico with some of his parishioners. He served churches in New Mexico as well as on the Llano Estacado. *Courtesy Christena Stephens.*

Later, he served as a priest in the Texas communities of Hereford, Bovina, St. Francis, Canadian, Stratford, White Deer, Lubbock, Friona, Dumas and Pep. In January 1969, Father Stanley became priest at the Holy Family Catholic Church in Nazareth, and during his thirteen years there, he wrote many of his books and helped Nazareth become incorporated in 1973.

On his days off, he conducted research at nearby Canyon's West Texas A&M University Library or the archives of the Panhandle-Plains Museum. He even on many occasions used his visits to Lubbock to do research at the Southwest Collection at Texas Tech University. These singular research days became sacred to him, as they are with many historians.

Although penniless, he often financed his own printings. Never tiring in his passion, he spent his vacations in small western towns gathering research materials for his books. A big part of Father Stanley's research was done by visiting the older residents of the communities he wrote about.

Father Stanley outlined and wrote most of his stories in blue ink in spiral-bound notebooks before he transferred them to typewritten manuscripts. Most of his typewritten manuscripts are incredibly spotless of errors.

Over time, he wrote 177 books and pamphlets that chronicled the history of many towns in the Texas Panhandle and New Mexico. Many record the history of the local Catholic churches or missions. He also wrote about the beginnings of Albuquerque and about the famous bandit Black Jack Ketchum. He told of the emerging cattle industry in The Texas Panhandle in *Cattlemen to Feed Lots (1880–1970)*, and about Taiban, New Mexico, a small village located on the western edge of the Llano Estacado.

Many of his readers assumed that the name F. Stanley was an abbreviation for Father Stanley. In reality, it was Francis Stanley, and he chose the pen name because Crocchiola was too hard for people to pronounce or spell. In the end, his heart was stolen by the history of Texas Panhandle and eastern New Mexico—the Llano Estacado. He was one who saw the wealth of its history that many never considered. Father Stanley Crocchiola died in 1996 at the age of eighty-seven and was buried at the Nazareth cemetery.

MENNONITES ON THE LLANO ESTACADO, PART I

Tina Siemens

West Texas and the Llano Estacado have always been home to many interesting people and events. But what many people don't know is that the Llano has connections to Netherlands, Poland, Ukraine and Canada. Thanks to these connections, reporters from all over the country flocked to this area to capture an international scene played out in the late 1970s.

The story the reporters followed began in the 1500s with a Roman Catholic priest named Menno Simons. After rejecting some of the practices and beliefs of the Roman Catholic Church, Menno Simons joined a group of Anabaptists. He soon had his own following in the Netherlands that became known as the Mennonites, the name taken from his first name. Ousted from place to place, his group moved to Prussia (present-day Poland), southern Russia (present-day Ukraine) and then to Canada.

At each location, the government promised the Mennonites autonomy in exchange for land they could work and develop. They lived up to their end of the bargain so successfully that their population grew to the point they needed more land. But often, privileges were taken away or changed, and members of the group were threatened or killed. Eventually, they moved on to new places.

In 1922, more than five thousand Mennonites left Canada for Mexico in six long trains, bringing with them animals, furniture, tools and grain.

A Mennonite school in Mexico. *Courtesy Tina Siemens.*

The journey ended at a large piece of land in the Bustillos Valley near Cuauhtémoc in the state of Chihuahua. As had happened in all countries they lived before, the president of Mexico signed a document guaranteeing them religious freedom, their own monetary system and exemption from service in the military. For the Mennonites, being left alone in their closed society was as close to heaven on earth as they could get.

It took many years to turn the rocky desert into a land that could sustain them. At first, starvation and death were ever-present, but eventually they persevered. The Bustillos Valley was a hard place, but their success meant not going hungry. There was little money for extravagances, but that mattered little because the Mennonites believed that suffering brought them closer to God.

Over the years, their population exploded. Because they did not believe in birth control, many women had twelve to eighteen children. Some babies died from disease because the Mennonites had no physicians, only self-taught laymen, whom they called village doctors, for healthcare. One sick child often passed a disease to another simply by visiting the common water pump.

The extremely frugal Mennonites even reused names. If a child named John died, the family's next boy born was named John. It was also an honor system to reuse the names of grandparents and aunts and uncles, as well as biblical names. Despite frequent deaths, families of ten living children were very common.

As newlyweds started their own families, they searched for land. Unfortunately, the local citizens in Mexico were not willing to sell. For the Mennonites, their entire life was in this land. What little money they had was hidden in their houses. For many, the friction between them and the native Mexicans was becoming more frequent.

One man saw a way out of all this: Jacob Rempel, of one of the original Mennonite families who moved from Canada. He silently questioned everything, including the poor educational system of the Mennonites. Mennonites were taught to read through a simple primer. After mastering that, they were given a booklet of the catechism, followed by studies in the New Testament and then the Old Testament. Mathematics included only basic addition and subtraction—no doubt to the joy of many students who never had to face the horrors of algebra, geometry and trigonometry.

Jacob knew that he lacked knowledge. The Mennonite Church leaders were the only ones who would negotiate with government entities over land contracts, privileges and other legal matters. As Jacob grew older and had children, his eldest son, also named Jacob, became a preacher.

Even though young Jacob had become indoctrinated, Jacob Sr. continued to question the reasons behind the harsh rules. For example, one rule required the removal of rubber tires from tractors, and burning them, replacing them with welded metal spokes onto the wheels. This caused the tractor to go slow and roughly through the fields. Jacob could not plow much land with the tractor. But that was the point—their faith taught them that suffering was good; it brings you closer to God and eliminates your free time, where so many men get into trouble.

When his son had a son, Jacob, now a grandfather, secretly lifted the newborn, named David, to his lips and whispered, "You will leave this place. I will help you find a way."

MENNONITES ON THE LLANO ESTACADO, PART 2

Tina Siemens

leeing from Canada to Mexico, Mennonites eventually found life harder in their new home in Chihuahua. With limited education and available land running out, keeping a family fed became difficult. These difficulties led David Rempel, the eldest son of Jacob Rempel the younger, to seek a path of escape his grandfather Jacob had promised him at birth. Yet leaving a Mennonite colony was not easy.

First, family ties were strong. Pressure from relatives intensified as soon as they caught wind of the discontent. If David and his family left and then returned, they would certainly face a rough life of isolation and disdain. Excommunication was always a possibility.

Next, raising the money to leave was almost impossible. Every penny went into food, clothing or shelter. The only way to raise a large sum was to sell everything. However, such action would tip off the colony, which in turn would trigger pressure to stay.

Finally, where could a Low German–speaking Mennonite with little education go? To another Mennonite colony? Or brave the big wide world and try an "Englander" city? So many hurdles, yet David Rempel was determined to overcome them. In 1974, he decided to move his wife and children to Paraguay, which he felt offered the best option.

Paraguay already had established Mennonite colonies. David's father, Jacob, owned land there. David hoped to live on it until he could get some of his own. With his father's reluctant blessing, he quietly sold a few assets to raise some money. Then, he crammed his family's belongings into a shipping container and dispatched it ahead to Tampico, hoping to slip out of the colony without too much drama. But before he could leave, a letter arrived in Mexico, addressed to David's father.

Someone in Paraguay had heard that David owned a motor vehicle, which was true. He had a beat-up Volkswagen Beetle parked in his barn. For Mennonites, owning a car was a major sin. It made life easy and helped the work go faster. But the religious authority in Paraguay told his father that David was not welcome there. And if he came, he might find life very difficult. Any relationships with Mennonites would be nonexistent.

David had no choice but to take a bus to the port at Tampico, Mexico, to reclaim his family possessions. After spending hard-earned money to get there, he found the shipping container and managed to turn it around. Once home, he regrouped.

But he did not give up. Next on his list was Canada, where there were still remnants of Mennonites who had not moved to Mexico. Supposedly, they were more liberal. David then took his family to Canada, hoping to gain citizenship, but because he and his Mennonite guide lacked knowledge about the outside world, they threw away the application papers that would have granted them citizenship. When their visa expired, they had to exit the country immediately. It was back to Mexico once again.

The Rempel Farm in Chihuahua, Mexico. *Courtesy Tina Siemens.*

After rebuilding his savings again, David targeted another place that he had heard of: the West Texas town of Seminole. There, it was reported that Mennonite farmers bought tractors and parts from local dealers located in Seminole. David decided to check it out himself.

After a quick visit to Seminole, David returned to Mexico full of incredible stories. He saw clothes that washed and dried themselves in magical machines. He saw that citizens there even built small houses for their dogs! David could not stop gushing about this land of milk and honey and knew that he had to find a way to escape to Seminole.

In 1976, David learned that U.S. citizenship was guaranteed to anyone who owned at least one acre of land. Soon, he and several other men organized a large group to buy a tract of land near Seminole. They raised a staggering $295,000, enough to make a down payment on 1,200 acres of land. Suddenly, hundreds of Mennonites wanted to leave Mexico, and all of them bought at least one acre of land. After all the years of failure for David, he hoped it would be a way out of Mexico for good.

In early 1977, David and his followers, now a sizable group, reached the U.S. border, excited about reaching their new home. Yet they discovered that the lawyer with their applications wasn't there to meet them. For five long days, the Mennonite men stood vigil in and around the immigration center, while their families waited in a cheap motel in Juarez.

On the last day, near closing time, one of the border agents found a way to communicate with David Rempel, who then explained their situation. The agent miraculously decided to grant them a temporary visa, which would allow them ninety days to sort out their problems. But he also learned that owning an acre of land did *not* entitle one to citizenship.

As they crossed the border, David was both excited and scared. But when he crested a rise and the lights of Seminole came into view, he told his family in a voice dripping with emotion, "We're home. Now, we're home!"

But could they stay?

MENNONITES ON THE LLANO ESTACADO, PART 3

Tina Siemens

Even though the Mennonite colony in Mexico had been there for more than fifty years, life was still hard. In 1977, more than five hundred Mennonites chose to join with my father, David Rempel, in seeking a new life near Seminole, Texas. As a prominent member of the Mennonite community, and with his grandfather secretly pushing him on, he brought me and our family to the United States. But could we stay?

Once in Seminole, our leaders pooled their funds to hire the best legal talent they could find, but there never seemed to be enough money for them. Then there were issues over the land. Because our leaders lacked an understanding of the ways of the world, they had not obtained water rights to the land they had bought. Planting crops in a semi-arid region without water was a foolish proposition. The real estate agent who handled the transaction assured everyone that the Mennonites understood they were not getting the water rights when they signed the complicated papers written in English.

Seeing his money drain from his pockets, David needed a job, and speaking Low German was not an asset when seeking employment in West Texas. But somehow, God smiled on him, granting him both a day and night job. He made money by wading into a raw sewage lagoon and setting pipes. The idea was to capture the raw sewage and use it for irrigating cotton fields. He also found work hoeing weeds in the hot Texas sun—not for himself, but rather for his three young children, including myself.

Even though we should have been in school, the family needed the money. Each dawn, my older brother David, sister Elizabeth and I trudged out to the fields for ten solid hours of hoeing endless rows of cotton. When it was time to get paid, our father collected the wages to buy the bare necessities, and the rest was paid toward the hopeful path to citizenship.

Soon, Border Patrol buses arrived to collect the Mennonites and take them back to Mexico. Expulsion would mean forfeiture of their land. Meanwhile, a second group of Mennonites came from Canada and paid a down payment of $445,000 for 6,400 acres, eighteen miles southwest of Seminole—but once again without water rights. The situation seemed hopeless, and it appeared that all would be lost.

But Seminole mayor Bob Clark intervened. After watching the Mennonites gather around the real estate agent's office each day, he decided to investigate. After he learned what was going on, he contacted longtime congressman George H. Mahon. As the chairman of the Ways and Means Committee, he was the point man for spending the government's money. And his district just happened to include Seminole, Texas.

Eventually, newspapers learned of the drama taking place in West Texas; almost overnight, reporters and cameramen were combing the streets of Seminole, interviewing witnesses and probing for every detail. One fact they uncovered was the Mennonites' refusal to accept charity. Even the tiny church they set up, which by law

Mennonite Girl Closes Her Eyes in Prayer
Schoolmates Have Ridiculed Sect's Children

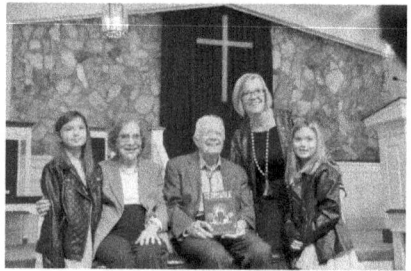

Top: This picture of Katharina Rempel (*left*) and her praying friend Tina Froese, which appeared in the June 8, 1979 issue of the *Albuquerque Journal*, helped call national attention to the plight of the Mennonites in their struggle to keep their land. *Clipping courtesy Tina Siemens and newspapers.com.*

Bottom: Tina Siemens and her granddaughters present former president Jimmy Carter and wife, Rosalynn, a memento of the Seminole, Texas community in 2019. *Courtesy Tina Siemens.*

could avoid paying property taxes, paid its fair share. There the Mennonites prayed to God for help, and it came in the form of one photo.

This one picture depicted eight-year-old girls sitting on benches, leaning forward, praying to God for help. With their blonde hair braided over their shoulders and blue eyes peering over tented hands, this image exploded onto the front pages of the country's major newspapers. When Americans read how the Mennonites simply wanted to worship God, work hard and be left alone, as well as how they had been deceived in the land deals, the country's outrage spread to senators and congressmen.

Both senators from Texas—John Tower and Lloyd Bentsen—sprang into action. With Mayor Clark holding a local vigil, guiding the press as they snapped photos for the continuing string of news articles, the Mennonites' prospects looked good. But then their visas ran out. Once again, they faced having to leave, but a miracle came in the form of the renewal of their visas.

Finally, in 1981, after four long years of uncertain existence, both houses of Congress passed laws granting pathway to citizenship to more than five hundred Mennonites. When President Jimmy Carter signed it, the Mennonites were granted green cards. And five years later, the entire group, including myself and my family, were sworn in as U.S. citizens.

Since that time, the ranks of the Texas Mennonites have expanded. God blessed them and their land. Out of nothing, the land has produced abundance, helping make Gaines County one of the most productive agricultural counties in the United States. But not all Mennonites are farmers, including my husband, John Siemens, who owns a thriving construction business and employs more than two dozen workers.

On November 11, 2019, I flew to Plains, Georgia, to visit former president Jimmy Carter and personally offer our thanks for his help. As a former peanut farmer, President Carter said that he loved helping the Mennonites, especially when he found out they were peanut farmers too.

PART V

SOMETHING OLD, SOMETHING NEW

The 2020–21 pandemic, while being caused by a novel virus, was not the first disease outbreak to stifle the nation. In 1918, the so-called Spanish influenza epidemic raced around the world and claimed nearly 700,000 lives across the United States. The Llano Estacado was not spared, as entire families suffered from the impact of the flu. Elissa Stroman's essay turns to oral history sources to tell the story of how people helped one another survive.

Two essays here recount how two entities—a town and a historic Bible class—changed their names after many years had passed.

This section also features stories that tell how history got changed by misinterpretation; how an ethnic neighborhood evolved, only to be changed by a devastating tornado; and how an entire region—the Permian Basin—is changing due to new discoveries of oil reserves never before imagined.

AN HONEST HISTORY

Paul H. Carlson

I f the maxim "each generation of historians writes history in light of what is foremost in its mind" is true, history becomes transient, plastic and mutable. With a past that changes, how does one produce an honest history? Consider, for example, two photos of early Lubbock and its famous white-painted, two-and-a-half-story Nicolett Hotel.

Good evidence suggests that the images represent Lubbock when the little town spread over land currently east of I-27 across from the Lubbock Country Club. Over time, the photos, it seems, became incorrectly associated with the new Lubbock, established around the modern downtown square.

The first photo shows six men sitting on the ground, with one of them, the man on the far right, identified as J.B. Jones, an early surveyor of Lubbock County. In the near background, a shallow gash in the land runs through the tableau. In the far background, one can see the large Nicolett Hotel with its two-level porch and several other structures. The little town in 1890, according to the late Texas historian Seymour V. Connor, contained thirty-seven buildings and about fifty people.

The caption under a ubiquitous copy of the photo reads in part: "[T]he first picture of the Lubbock skyline; it was taken in 1892." The date seems to be in error. Less well-known copies of the same image show different dates—1889 in one and 1890 in another.

This picture of the Lubbock skyline has been labeled on different copies as 1889, 1890 and 1892. The two-story building at left is the Nicolett Hotel. *Courtesy Southwest Collection, Texas Tech University.*

Again, the photo shows the front porch with a top over the second-floor balcony. But after moving the big hotel, when they rebuilt the porch, builders did not replace the protective cover over the upper deck.

Rather than a "skyline view" of new Lubbock in 1892, the photo instead shows the little town and the Nicolett as they existed sometime before the end of February 1891, the month in which men with horses and mules pulled the large hotel minus its front porch about five miles south to modern downtown Lubbock.

The second photo offers more troublesome issues. It represents a front view of the Nicolett Hotel and shows thirty-four people standing and sitting on the upper and lower porches, with E.B. Green visible on horseback in the street before them.

The caption line attached to one copy of the photo reads in part: "The Nicolette [*sic*] Hotel, corner of Broadway and Avenue H [Buddy Holly Avenue], in 1895 or 1896." Because someone has identified many of the people in the image, one feels the person must be correct about the dates. Yet both the dates and the location seem wrong.

Most photographic evidence suggests that after the hotel's repositioning, workmen did not replace the upper-level cover over the porch or reattach the big Nicolett Hotel sign atop the second-story balcony. If true, the photo dates to before the end of February 1891, when owners relocated the hotel from its original spot east of the modern country club to the current

The date of this historic photo of the Nicolett may be earlier than thought. *Courtesy Southwest Collection, Texas Tech University.*

downtown square. In reality, a photographer probably took the image in late 1890 or very early 1891.

Built in late 1888 and early 1889, the Nicolett Hotel was an imposing structure with eighteen rooms. Frank E. Wheelock, manager of Lubbock County's IOA Ranch, and Rollie Burns, a cowboy and an early Lubbock chronicler, along with investors from Fort Worth, constructed the hotel, which Wheelock named for a similar business in Minneapolis.

At its original location on high ground about five miles north of the present-day Lubbock County Courthouse, the Nicolett quickly became a popular place. Its lobby was spacious and relaxing, its rooms peaceful and its dining room inviting. It attracted such overnight guests as "drummers," cattlemen, land agents and others, as well as local folks who sought a good meal.

Importantly, during the summer and fall of 1890, the hotel served as a conference room for members of rival villages (Lubbock and Monterey) who met over a period of several months to hammer out a compromise that created a new Lubbock. They finished in mid-December.

Early the next year, 1891, in a major undertaking, men led by Wheelock and Burns hauled the sizeable structure to its new site. The men took the Nicolett straight south. They inched it down a gentle grade into present

Mackenzie Park, crossed Yellow House Creek just below its junction with Blackwater Draw, edged it up a moderate slope out of the wide valley and headed it straight to the new site. They placed the hotel at the corner of South Singer and South First Street, now known as Broadway and Buddy Holly Avenue.

Until a few months later, after which the county had built its tall courthouse, the Nicolett stood as the leading symbol of sophisticated life along a moving edge of High Plains settlement. Clearly, for an honest history of early Lubbock and the Nicolett Hotel, some aspects of our city's 130-year-old past need reevaluation. The photo captions mentioned here may represent two of them.

AZTLAN PARK AND "MEXICAN TOWN"

Jack Becker

On the site of Aztlan Park—located in east Lubbock and bounded by Buddy Holly Avenue, First Place, Avenue J and Cesar E. Chavez Drive—there is a historical marker commemorating an immigrant labor camp that once stood there. The camp, which may have preceded Lubbock by several years, went through several name changes as the residents' nationality and their occupations changed.

Itinerant cowboys lived at the site first in the early 1880s, stopping here as they traveled between ranches looking for work, or camped out there when not needed at local ranches. Many of them were Hispanic.

After the creation of Lubbock and the coming of the railroad in 1909, some railroad workers found temporary housing in the area. Since most of the railroad workers were from El Paso and Hispanic, the area became a Mexican enclave, although it was widely known as Shipley's Railroad Camp.

The arrival of the railroad prompted increased cotton production on the Llano Estacado. Ranch pastures became cotton fields, and with the transition, demand for seasonal workers increased. Farmers needed workers to cultivate and pick the cotton and, after harvest, to work in area gins.

Soon, seasonal workers came annually with their families from south Texas or Mexico. Consequently, the railroad labor camp became a migrant workers enclave and became known locally as "Mexican Town," the "Chihuahua District" or simply "the Barrio." As the number of seasonal

Two young residents of the migrant camp at the site of Atzlan Park in east Lubbock pose in front of a migrant *truckero*, date unknown. *Courtesy Christie Martinez.*

workers increased and the size of "Mexican Town" grew, the area took on a more permanent appearance.

Living conditions, however, remained poor, as immigrant workers lived in tents or huts made out of any kind of material they could find. The streets remained unpaved and sanitation conditions terrible. Due to overcrowding and the squalid living conditions, outbreaks of measles, smallpox, dysentery and diphtheria became an all-too-familiar occurrence. The onset of the Great Depression only made living conditions worse in the camp.

During World War II, as young men joined the armed services or left the farm or ranch to work in defense plants, a shortage of labor for agricultural work became critical. To help solve this problem, the federal government signed an agreement with Mexico in 1942 to allow a massive influx of Mexican workers; it became known as the Bracero Program. Through the Bracero Program, hundreds of thousands of Mexican workers came to the United States to harvest crops. Some found their way to Lubbock.

Every fall, hundreds of workers came to the South Plains to harvest the area's cotton. Downtown merchants soon learned to take advantage of the economic boom they brought to Lubbock. Every Saturday during the cotton harvest, workers flooded downtown Lubbock to shop and socialize. Many came from area labor camps, while others lived in "Mexican Town," which was now surrounded by the Guadalupe neighborhood.

To make it easier for local farmers to find workers, in 1948, Lubbock's city council or perhaps the Texas Employment Commission erected a corrugated metal building in the Barrio that served as a labor recruiting site. It became the location where workers could wait to be hired and where farmers could find a dependable source of labor.

Because Lubbock remained segregated well into the 1960s, opportunities were limited for immigrant workers to find jobs or participate in activities outside the Barrio. But with every challenge comes an opportunity. Innovative residents of the camp opened restaurants, a movie theater, a barbershop and other commercial establishments. A Catholic church and school soon followed.

On May 11, 1970, a tornado struck Lubbock, killing twenty-six people and destroying more than 1,100 homes. Half of the people who died had lived in the Guadalupe neighborhood, where the labor camp and half of its homes were demolished by the storm. The extensive damage to the area was due in part to the flimsy construction of the homes, composed mostly of wood and stucco. But the aftermath of the tornado led to many Mexican workers finding jobs cleaning up debris and working on rebuilding Lubbock.

Due to the extensive damage and the amount of federal dollars made available after the storm, the City of Lubbock launched an extensive plan of urban renewal, focused primarily on the Guadalupe neighborhood, leveling buildings that remained standing; moving residents to better, safer and more modern housing; and constructing a new Civic Center on the site of the old neighborhood.

MONROE AND NEW DEAL

Sandy Fortenberry

L ike many South Plains communities, the story of New Deal, which is located ten miles north of Lubbock on Interstate 27, began with the arrival of a railroad. Unlike most towns, it changed names as it grew.

New Deal began as Monroe, a junction on the 1909 extension of the Santa Fe Railroad from Plainview to Lubbock. Towns along the railroads were often named for those who gave financial support or influence for rail construction. Monroe G. and Mollie Abernathy were an influential Lubbock couple who supported the extension of the Santa Fe because they knew it would be vital to the city's growth and prosperity. In return for their support, C.M. Ward, a Santa Fe official, invited Mollie Abernathy to name two new towns on the line, and she chose "Abernathy" and "Monroe" to honor her husband.

With the coming of the railroad, boosters began promoting land and settlement adjacent to the new line. Frank Bowles, who came to the Lubbock area around 1890, was actively involved in land promotion. Records from the Texas General Land Office indicate that he purchased Section 28, Block D (640 acres), from the state in 1909. Bowles recorded a plat for the town of Monroe on 160 acres in the southwest quarter (SW¼) of the section. The survey laid out forty-four blocks further divided into lots, with the rail line running along the west side of the townsite.

By December 1909, Bowles's new town of Monroe had a rail depot but little else. Unfortunately for Bowles, the town of Monroe did not develop as he visualized. In hindsight, he should have situated his town west of the railroad, not on the east side, in order to take advantage of both rail and wagon/automobile traffic on the main road between Lubbock and Plainview and Amarillo, designated State Highway 9 in 1917. Early Monroe resident Ward Crim recognized the advantage and in 1925 platted the southeast corner portion of his land west of the railroad as the Ward Crim Addition to the Monroe Townsite. By then, automobile and truck traffic had eclipsed the railroad in importance.

The main road, Highway 9, often called the Amarillo Highway, was designated U.S. 385 in 1926, paved through Monroe by 1931 and became U.S. 87 in 1935. As a result, by the late 1920s, the town had a school, a Methodist church, a general store, a blacksmith shop, cotton gins, a café and a lumberyard, most located west of the Santa Fe Railroad.

On May 28, 1917, Monroe became the Monroe Common School District no. 10 of the Lubbock County Schools. One month later, its residents voted to build a two-story brick building with two school rooms and an auditorium. Then, in 1935, Lubbock County formed six rural high schools by action of the County School Board, consolidating Monroe School with Caldwell, Grovesville and Center into New Deal Rural High School District no. 3. The grouping occurred during President Franklin Roosevelt's administration of the "New Deal Policies," resulting in the name New Deal for the new district. A new elementary school was built in 1938, after the 1917 brick building burned. The campus grew with a new high school in 1966.

In its beginning, Monroe served as a farming community. J.V. Daniell built Monroe's first gin, and by the 1930s, it had two gins, three churches, three grocery stores and three service stations. In 1948, its citizens petitioned U.S. Representative George Mahon for a post office, but because there was another Monroe, Texas postal facility, the Postal Department chose the name New Deal. On June 1, 1949, Monroe officially became New Deal with the establishment of the new post office.

On June 13, 1970, New Deal residents voted to incorporate about seven hundred acres along both sides of the proposed interstate highway. A local farmer, Billy Fortenberry, became the first mayor, and the first aldermen were David Williams, T.J. Attebury, Berhl Robertson, Bob Shropshire and Ray West. At the time, its population was approximately five hundred. In 1976, under the mayoral direction of Ray West, the town built a city hall. In 1977, residents created a volunteer fire department, which acquired its first fire truck from the county. In 1978, the city constructed two bays adjoining city hall for a fire station. A new fire/EMS station was built in 2014.

The Monroe School, circa 1921, was built in 1917 and expanded in 1924 to six classrooms and an auditorium. *Courtesy Sandy Fortenberry.*

Although the new Interstate 27, authorized by the Federal-Aid Highway Act of 1968, bypassed New Deal, its construction gave the little town four-lane freeway access to downtown Lubbock, prompting new growth. The community continues to prosper, with a population of almost seven hundred and a student enrollment of seven hundred in New Deal schools. Since incorporation, New Deal has increased the size of its city limits through various annexations. Started from dreams of early settlers and built by hardworking citizens, Monroe became a thriving community with a new name—New Deal.

SOUTH PLAINS VOICES OF THE 1918 INFLUENZA PANDEMIC

Elissa Stroman

The Southwest Collection/Special Collections Library at Texas Tech University has more than 6,500 oral history recordings, many of which are life history interviews of early settlers to this region that discuss various twentieth-century topics, including the 1918 Spanish flu.

Little historical research has been published regarding the impact the 1918 flu had on the Llano Estacado, but through these oral histories, we have a glimpse of the flu's lasting legacy. The flu hit Texas in late September and slowly expanded throughout the fall and winter.

Lubbock mayor C.E. Parks closed all schools and public gatherings between October 15 and November 2, 1918. Elsewhere on the South Plains, many schools shut down sometime around Thanksgiving and did not reopen until 1919. A common theme in interviews was that the flu spread because sick people traveled to other towns, taking the virus with them.

Our interviewees recall how quickly it ravaged less developed Texas boomtowns like Ranger and Thurber because of the diverse number of people living in proximity to one another. Yet the flu also spread steadily through the rural South Plains region. With many families living on small individual farms, interviewees recalled that they avoided the worst of the flu by self-quarantining and sustaining themselves on their own crops, making few trips to town.

At the time, Lubbock was a small but growing town, with two newly built hospitals: the West Texas Sanitarium in 1916 and the Lubbock Sanitarium in early 1918. At this time, doctors made house calls. Dr. M.C. Overton (owner of the land east of Texas Tech that now bears his name) worked around the clock when the flu hit; having an automobile driver enabled him to sleep in between house calls.

The underlying problem with the 1918 flu (as with early cases of COVID-19) was the lack of a reliable treatment. No shots or vaccines were available then to help slow the spread, keep the fevers down or relieve the headaches. There was no penicillin or sulfa drugs, and interviewees spoke of various treatments attempted (like aspirin or quinine) with varying levels of success. One man swore that he survived by eating a raw onion every morning for breakfast.

After working with malaria patients for years, one doctor treated patients with small doses of calomel (a mercury chloride mineral that is highly poisonous in large doses). Some tried cloths soaked in a menthol-like solution to cool the fevers. Others suggested adults drink a glass of milk with two tablespoons of whiskey.

In a 1980 interview, Mrs. C.G. Bloom recalled how in 1918 she found her six-month-old baby blue and lifeless from a fever three mornings in a row. But warm bath water mixed with a bit of whiskey revived her infant. In most cases, the only course of action was to stay in bed and sleep, opening windows and allowing in fresh air.

Often, entire families became infected; neighbors deposited food on front porches to ensure they had sustenance. Mothers took care of their children and households while simultaneously fighting the virus, frequently causing them to relapse or stay sick longer.

In the end, the worst flu cases turned into pneumonia. Then doctors were forced to insert a tube into patients' rib cages to drain the excessive fluids from their lungs. Others were fitted with thick, padded pneumonia jackets that kept their chests warm.

The year 1918 was a harsh time on the South Plains. A drought in the spring and an exceptionally hot summer was followed by a very hard winter. Many ranchers spent late 1918 tending to cattle to ensure that they did not freeze to death during the day, only to come home to families battling the flu.

Interviewees spoke of how the flu seemed to hit younger men the hardest. In 1978, Perry Everett described "big, stout men" who "you didn't think anything could kill them" often succumbed to the flu. Harry Kelley

The first class of nurses to graduate from the Lubbock Sanitarium pose in front of the hospital in 1918; they were among the first to deal with the influenza epidemic. *Courtesy Southwest Collection, Texas Tech University.*

remarked, "It seemed like the larger a person was, the more healthy they were, the more likely they'd go down with this thing."

Edith Courtney Sanders told a story of a Floydada boy who "took it and died right off." A bad blizzard combined with many deaths forced people in Floydada to use a sled to carry his casket to the cemetery. Five Floydada residents were buried on Christmas Day 1918. Interviews also mention how the Floydada courthouse became a hospital.

There is comfort in knowing that our forbearers survived a global pandemic under far worse conditions than we are experiencing, as they had to deal with poor weather compounded with lack of medical advancements or other technological resources.

Although most survivors of the 1918 flu pandemic are no longer alive, their voices live on in the Southwest Collection's oral history recordings, a testament to the resiliency of West Texans. Together, we can work to take care of one another.

THE DOWNTOWN BIBLE CLASS

INTERDENOMINATIONAL CHRISTIANS TOGETHER

Jack Becker

T he Downtown Bible Class started life as the Men's Downtown Bible Class in 1928, sponsored by the First Baptist Church of Lubbock in an effort to reach out to businessmen, as well as traveling salesmen who found themselves in Lubbock over the weekend. Lubbock in 1928 was a fast-growing town of twenty thousand; business was booming, and many salesmen found it profitable to stop in Lubbock's downtown business district.

The Bible Class originated with Dr. W.T. White, who became the pastor of First Baptist in March 1928. One of his first tasks after arriving at First Baptist was to organize an interdenominational Sunday school class for men. He envisioned the class as an autonomous, self-financing entity to be located near the downtown business area.

White enlisted the help of three dynamic men to help him with the project: Professor E.W. Provence, a Texas Technological College professor; O.W. English, a local doctor; and O.W. McLeod, a businessman. The men picked the Lyric Theater on the 1100 block of Texas Avenue as a place to meet, and the class met there for the first time in August 1928. As hoped, many of the first attendees were traveling businessmen. Due to the class's location and the spirit of its early members, the class grew rapidly.

By late 1933, the class had outgrown the Lyric Theater and two years later moved into the Palace Theater on Main Street and Avenue J, a building with modern cooling and central heating. Despite a growing economic

Members of the Men's Downtown Bible Class gather near the Lyric Theater for a picture on April 28, 1929. *Courtesy Downtown Bible Class.*

depression, the class continued to expand, aided by its weekly broadcast on radio station KFYO.

During the Depression, the Bible Class helped destitute families through its Family Help Program and also supported Buckner's Children Home and the Salvation Army. The Family Help Program became so large and the need so great that the class hired a social worker to help with the program. During World War II, the class helped sponsor programs for service men and women stationed at Reese Army Air Field.

E.N. Jones, president of Texas Tech, also became president of the class in 1953, and the class entered a new period of prominence and growth. With Jones as president, some of the most influential men in Lubbock joined the class. Also, two dynamic teachers lent it more credibility: Roy Bass, who later became mayor of Lubbock, and George McClesky, who taught the class for more than fourteen years (August 1958–September 1972). Both men were highly popular and effective teachers, and due to their highly skillful teaching, attendance grew to more than four hundred but then began to sag.

In 1981, the class moved to the Scottish Rite Temple on Sixth Street and Avenue Q, which helped to boost attendance once again. Changes continued in the 1980s when John Ballard became the new teacher. An assistant pastor at First Baptist, Ballard taught the class for more than thirty-five years until he retired in 2017. Ballard's positive and sunny disposition, energy and sense of humor endeared him to members. But despite Ballard's best efforts, attendance slipped even further as Lubbock grew to the southwest, away from the city center.

In the early 1990s, the class voted to allow women to join. Many had been attending for some time as guests, and when extended membership, those and many more enrolled; by 2001, women made up 43 percent of the class. With women as class members, a change in name was in order. The class, known as the Men's Downtown Bible Class for almost sixty-four years, became the Downtown Bible Class. In 2011, Quatha Baker became the class's first woman president.

As much as the class liked meeting in the Scottish Rite Temple, the class found it necessary to move again and relocated to the old Presbyterian church in downtown Lubbock in 2007. In 2019, it moved to its present location at the Yellowhouse Masonic Lodge No. 841, located on 5015 Gary Avenue in southwest Lubbock. Reverend Calvin Gray serves as its teacher.

Over the years, the Downtown Bible Class has expanded its giving to include support for Wayland Baptist University, the Lubbock State School, Gideons International, Texas Boy's Ranch, mission work in Japan and other charities. Along the way, the class has changed the emphasis of its radio ministry to become an outreach program for shut-ins. Throughout its more than ninety years of ministry, the class has consistently taught the Bible and put its teachings into practice by reaching out to help others. Although it is no longer located in downtown Lubbock, it certainly remains in the heart of Lubbock.

THE WOLFCAMP SHALE "GOLD RUSH" IN THE PERMIAN BASIN

Paul V. Chaplo

My pilot and I took off from Midland, Texas, in a single-engine Cessna aircraft to capture the Permian Basin and some historic sites in aerial photographs for my upcoming book and traveling exhibition *Amarillo Flights: Aerial Views of Llano Estacado Country*. I could see a grid of oil wells filling the vista below the puffy clouds of the West Texas blue sky and went to work with my two cameras. Although I work as an oil field photographer, my later research to write captions led to some eye-opening information, and soon I found myself infected with a "West Texas crude" version of gold fever.

In the light of a recent U.S. Geological Survey report, the immensity of the underground petroleum resources is even more staggering than previously thought. A new shale oil and natural gas boom in the western part of the region known as the Wolfcamp Shale of the Delaware Basin is currently underway.

Beneath this flat land is a hidden terrain and geologic timeline that dizzy our comprehension. It's hard to imagine that this locale was once the edge of a rich ancient sea, when its parallel likely laid along the earth's equator. The Permian Basin is a 250-mile-wide and 300-mile-long underground continental basin that stretches across West Texas and southeastern New Mexico. Named for the Permian period, about 250 million years ago, when most of the sediment filled the basin, the base geology resulted from tectonic events during Precambrian times more than 800 million years ago.

The basin is not a homogeneous bowl but rather a matrix of complex underground geologic structures and different sediment histories and sub-basins that have created multiple levels of rich oil and natural gas deposits. At its deepest point, the sediment reaches five miles. In scenes akin to the *Beverly Hillbillies* television show, early ranchers discovered oil and gas traces as they drilled for water.

In 2018, the U.S. Geological Survey reevaluated the size of the reserve and determined that the natural gas resources were 1,700 percent of the previous estimate. The western part of the Permian Basin—the Wolfcamp Shale and overlying Bone Spring Formation in the Delaware Basin—also contains about 281 trillion cubic feet of natural gas, 46.3 billion barrels of oil and 20 billion barrels of natural gas liquids.

Advances in extraction techniques make each well more productive. Horizontal drilling now allows the bore hole to be directed sideways for more than two miles. Fracking uses high-pressure water, chemicals and carbon dioxide to fracture the porous but dense rock. One bore hole can now access up to seventy zones and extract resources from each. The bottleneck for the current 3.8 million gallons of crude oil produced daily is pipeline capacity—a problem being resolved by several new pipeline projects.

It is widely acknowledged that the world's largest conventional onshore oil field is the Saudi Ghawar. In early 2019, in a historic moment, the Permian Basin exceeded production from the Gwahar. Due to secrecy, it is unclear if the Saudis have been reducing production to conserve reserves. That being said, the prominence of the Permian Basin in the world energy market is undeniable. The scale of the Permian reserves, paired with efficient operating costs, make it likely that any attempted OPEC oil price wars directed against U.S. shale oil such will fail just like the one that failed in 2016, when the instigators suffered economically.

Meanwhile, after some "bust" years, there is a new boom in the Permian Basin, and places like Midland and Odessa are brimming with well-paid oil workers and trucks hauling equipment, water, sand and oil. Places farther west such as Pecos, Texas, are hopping like gold rush camps. In a modern version of the cowboy blow-off towns of the Old West, workers with pockets full of cash find the usual vices, although drugs like meth now accompany a hard drink. Due to fatality accidents often involving oil field trucks and sleep-deprived drivers, the stretch of Highway 285 that runs through Pecos, Texas, and Carlsbad, New Mexico, has been nicknamed

Permian Basin oil well locations and service roads form a grid when seen from the air. *Courtesy Paul Chaplo.*

the "Highway of Death." Drilling rigs that once sat rusting in rows are back in the field. Prices for lodging have skyrocketed.

As I finish this article, I am packing my camera gear and heading to Pecos to photograph portraits of petroleum executives on drilling locations for their website. I hope to get some brisket for lunch before they run out at the local BBQ joint, as they do every day. As an oil executive once told me, "The prettiest sight in West Texas is a pump jack going up and down." The hardworking people who make a living in the Permian "oil patch" agree. That includes me.

PART VI

FROM THE FRYING PAN TO THE FLAG

Amarillo anchors the northern end of the Llano Estacado, and the area boasts the same colorful history as that of the Lubbock-dominated southern region. In this section, you will meet the first woman rancher of the upper Texas Panhandle, one who chose a life of ranching after losing her minister husband. Also in this chapter, Amarillo takes center stage, with essays on the nearby Frying Pan Ranch and that of a brutal murder that prompted the city to begin greater pursuit of law and order. Another story focuses on the role of Amarillo resident Lucille Shields in the national movement for women's voting rights; the final two document World War II contributions of West Texas State Teachers' College and the reluctant move toward integration at that school in the 1950s.

THE FRYING PAN RANCH

H. Allen Anderson

One of the most successful cattle enterprises in West Texas during the height of the 1880s "Beef Bonanza" was the Frying Pan Ranch, established by Henry B. Sanborn, a sales representative for Joseph F. Glidden's barbed wire manufacturing firm in DeKalb, Illinois. An owner of a successful ranch in Grayson County, Texas, Sanborn sought to further advertise his new product at his new ranch.

In 1881, acting in partnership with Glidden, Sanborn purchased ninety-five sections of choice Panhandle land covering the southwestern portion of Potter County from about the Canadian River down into northwestern Randall County. The tract included Tecovas Spring, once a trading site for Indians and Comancheros and subsequently utilized as a watering place by *pastores* from New Mexico for their flocks of sheep. John Summerfield, surveyor for the Gunter & Munson firm of Sherman, Texas, reported the spring's constant flow of fresh water to Sanborn, who then chose the site for his ranch headquarters.

The story goes that when Sanborn initially picked his ranch's brand, he created a brand in the shape of a panhandle. When a cowhand saw it, he reportedly remarked, "Why that's a skillet—a fryin' pan!" Hence the name.

After buying the land, Sanborn sought to enclose it in barbed wire and hired Warren W. Wetzel of Sherman, Texas, to oversee the task. At a cost of $39,000, Wetzel built the fence with cedar posts brought from both Palo Duro

Canyon and the breaks of the Sierrita de la Cruz in the ranch's northwestern portion. When completed, the four-wire fence covered 120 miles.

Wetzel stayed on as the ranch's bookkeeper and in 1882 brought his bride, Kate, from New York; for the next six years, she was the only woman in that part of Potter County and became a favorite among area cowboys. The Wetzels built a dugout in the hillside near Tecovas Spring that served as the Frying Pan headquarters until the completion of a large, nine-room adobe house and stalls nearby. Arch Childers, employed on Sanborn's Grayson County ranch, was hired as the Frying Pan's first foreman.

Before long, the Frying Pan had fifteen thousand head of cattle, and its owners added 125,000 more acres, including the present site of Wildorado in Oldham County. In 1884, Sanborn first visited his new ranch. His initial fears—that there "was not enough grass to feed a goose"—were promptly dispelled by his sight of some twenty thousand fattened cattle.

In 1887, the serene life of the Frying Pan was disrupted by the arrival of the Fort Worth & Denver City Railway, which laid its tracks diagonally across the ranch, cutting it into east and west pastures. With the organization of Potter County, Amarillo, which lay just to the east of the ranch, became its seat of government. As a result, Sanborn decided to develop townsites in the new fast-growing town.

With the influx of new businesses and residences, Sanborn and Glidden in 1892 opted to end their partnership, with Sanborn retaining his town properties and the Randall County land, while Glidden became the sole owner of the remainder of the Frying Pan Ranch properties.

According to their new agreement, Sanborn would run the ranch for two more years and make the $150,000 mortgage payment to Isaac L. Ellwood, Glidden's associate in the barbed wire business. By 1894, when the contract expired, Glidden and Sanborn had disposed of all the Frying Pan cattle, with Ellwood taking the three-year-olds, numbering about five thousand head. Subsequently, the ranch land was cut up into various pastures and leased out.

In 1898, Glidden transferred the Frying Pan to his son-in-law, William Henry Bush of Chicago, for $68,000. Later, Bush's half-brother, James A. Bush, became its manager in 1906. In 1908, the town of Bushland was established as a station on the Chicago, Rock Island & Gulf line about fourteen miles west of Amarillo.

Following the ranch's division and prior to 1920, W.H. and Ruth Bush built a new, more spacious ranch house, near Tecovas Spring, around which Ruth planted some trees. Later, it became the residence of the late Stanley

Six-room headquarters of the Frying Pan Ranch, also known as "The Adobe," 1881; it was located northwest of Amarillo. *Courtesy Southwest Collection, Texas Tech University.*

Marsh III and his wife, Wendy, a granddaughter of W.H. Bush; subsequently, Marsh dubbed the place "Toad Hall."

To this day, Bush heirs continue to manage the ranch properties, now known as the Bush Estate, and still use the Frying Pan brand. As for Tecovas Spring, the old stone springhouse bears a memorial plaque as a tribute to the early days. Amarillo's Western Avenue runs along the ranch's original eastern boundary. Like the Spade Ranches farther south in the Lubbock area established by Ellwood, the Frying Pan truly was one ranch that was built on barbed wire.

MARY JANE ALEXANDER

THE FIRST WOMAN RANCHER IN THE PANHANDLE

Jean Stuntz

In 1885, Mary Jane Alexander; her husband, Reverend C.W. Alexander; and their five children moved from Sherman to Mobeetie, Texas. Reverend Alexander had been asked to start a new Presbyterian church in the Wild West town in the eastern Panhandle. As the family journeyed there, while they tried to cross the flooded Pease River, a large tree hit their wagon.

Reverend Alexander and Mary Jane were both thrown out of the wagon and into the river. Fortunately, C.W. was upstream, and although he went under water, the current pushed him into the horses and he was able to use their harnesses to pull himself back up. Mary Jane was holding their baby but managed to grab onto the wagon tongue and keep both their heads above water.

They survived the disaster, but it took a heavy toll. After arriving at Mobeetie, the Alexanders moved into a small house, and C.W. began his ministry, which took him all around the eastern Panhandle. One night, he was caught in a freezing rain, and that, combined with the water that had gotten into his lungs during his plunge into the Pease River, caused his death in 1885. Mary Jane was left a widow at forty-six with five children in a place where she had few friends and no relatives.

While most women in this position would have quickly remarried or moved back east, Mary Jane instead filed for homestead on one section of land and bought an adjoining section on Washita Creek near the border with Indian Territory. This was the beginning of the Alexander Ranch.

Mary Jane Alexander, circa 1927, two years before her death in 1929. *Courtesy Panhandle-Plains Historical Museum.*

She and her children struggled to survive, gathering wild grasses to sell to the soldiers in Fort Elliott as hay. They also harvested wild sand plums, which she made into jelly for the soldiers and the people of Mobeetie, utilizing empty whiskey bottles gathered from around the saloon tents in Mobeetie and turning them into jelly jars.

Her sons gathered bones left by the buffalo hunters and took them to Dodge City, Kansas, to sell. The second-youngest son, R.T., at the age of fourteen, became a freighter, carrying supplies from Wheeler County to Dodge City and back again.

The family was always on the lookout for unbranded cattle that had strayed from nearby ranches. The ranch owners and managers all admired and respected Mary Jane and allowed her sons to claim these calves as their own.

Cowboys came to visit often, both to get a home-cooked meal and to teach some of their skills to the Alexander family. Mary Jane was always ready to whip up another pan of biscuits for the young men. As R.T. grew up, he studied animal husbandry and bred the strays he found into a magnificent herd of Herefords.

Neighbors described Mary Jane as a very religious woman who was known for her hospitality and determination to give her children a better life. She educated all her children at Polk College in Missouri. Her eldest son, Hugh, became a Presbyterian minister like his father; second son R.T. became a respected rancher; and the third son, Erastus, became a doctor. Her two daughters were also college educated, with Nona becoming a teacher until she married and Lucy becoming a missionary to China.

When Nona married and moved to nearby Canadian, Texas, Mary Jane went with her. Here, too, she was widely respected for her piety, charity and kindness. When it became obvious that she was nearing her end, people came from all over to say goodbye, to tell her how much they appreciated all the things she had done for them. She died in 1929.

In 1961, the Panhandle-Plains Museum in Canyon recognized her for being the first woman rancher in the Texas Panhandle, and her family donated papers and other material to its Research Center, as well as funds to establish a gallery to honor Panhandle pioneers. Then, in 1991 the Texas Family Land Heritage Program recognized Mary Jane and her descendants for being the longest continually operating, family-owned ranch in Hemphill County.

Mary Jane Alexander epitomizes the Texas pioneer woman. She centered her life on family, her faith and her community. She was hardworking, resourceful and generous. Women like her made the Panhandle and Llano Estacado communities the amazing places they are today.

THE PANHANDLE SUPPORTED WOMAN'S SUFFRAGE

Marty Kuhlman

In 2020, Americans celebrated the 100th anniversary of the Nineteenth Amendment extending the right to vote to women, a movement that had beginnings in Texas in 1868 and received support from Panhandle women as early as 1902.

The first mention of women being given the vote in Texas was in 1868 at the state's constitutional convention when T.H. Mundane put forward a resolution that qualified citizens should be allowed to vote "without distinction of sex." Opposition quickly appeared, stating that women had an "inborn refinement" and should "shrink from the busy noise of election days," and the resolution died in committee.

The first organization dedicated to woman's suffrage in the state was the Texas Equal Rights Association, formed in 1893 with founding members being from East and South Texas. Suffragette Dr. Ellen Keller of Fort Worth gave a speech declaring that women should be "permitted to help make the laws that govern them."

The first group in the Panhandle to support woman's suffrage was the Woman's Christian Temperance Union (WCTU), which formed a chapter in Canadian in 1902. The motto of the WCTU was "the ballot in the hands of women is the surest and shortest way to prohibition." The chapter in Canadian spent most of its energy on working for the prohibition of alcohol but recognized that women should be allowed to vote.

Lucille Shields, Amarillo suffragette. *Courtesy Library of Congress.*

Only a few suffrage organizations were left in the state by 1912, and some were on college campuses like the University of Texas. But one Panhandle college had an Equal Suffrage League. A photograph of fourteen women making up the group appeared in the 1912 yearbook of West Texas State Normal College in Canyon. A poem under the picture declared that men have stolen and polluted the ballot and declared that only "Equal suffrage'll make it pure."

In March 1912, the *Randall County News* covered a debate between coeds on suffrage. A group of male students burst into the meeting carrying a banner reading, "We need protection." Others dressed up like old men carrying babies, implying that if women were given the vote, babies would be neglected and men would have to care for them. The evening ended when history professor and supporter of suffrage Margaret Cofer read the essay, "Shakespeare's Opinion on Woman's Suffrage."

By 1918, a suffragette organization had formed in Amarillo, and one of its residents, Lucille Shields, became a member of the National Woman's Party (NWP), a suffrage organization that utilized direct action such as picketing to win a national suffrage amendment.

Shields traveled to Washington, D.C., where she joined a demonstration on July 4, 1917. She and twelve other members marched in front of the White House and carried a banner with a quote from the Declaration of Independence: "GOVERNMENTS DERIVE THEIR JUST POWERS FROM THE CONSENT OF THE GOVERNED." Police officers stopped the march and arrested the demonstrators for "blocking traffic." The judge handed down a sentence of three days in jail or a twenty-five-dollar fine. The women all chose the three days in jail to bring publicity to their cause.

Shields also participated in "watchfire demonstrations," the burning of President Woodrow Wilson's speeches in front of the White House. Protesters accused Wilson of hypocrisy since he spoke of spreading democracy while women in the United States could not vote. Burning the speeches led to Shields spending another five days in jail.

While Shields struggled for a national amendment, others continued to fight in the state. The Texas legislature had given women the right to vote in state primaries by 1918, but women could not vote in all elections.

In May 1919, male voters turned down an equal suffrage amendment, 54 percent to 46 percent.

A number of western states had passed state suffrage amendments—Colorado in 1893, Kansas in 1912 and Oklahoma in 1918. Concerning woman's suffrage, Panhandle residents had more in common with neighboring states than with most regions of Texas, best reflected by the fact that Panhandle voters supported a state woman's suffrage amendment with 4,582 votes (or 66 percent) for and 2,320 (or 34 percent) opposed. Out of twenty-five Panhandle counties (Moore County did not hold an election), all but Hutchison supported the amendment. East Texas opposed the amendment at 54 percent to 46 percent, while South Texas voted 61 percent to 39 percent against suffrage.

No matter how the state voted, the following week, in May 1919, the U.S. House of Representatives passed a national amendment calling for woman's suffrage.

The Panhandle continued to show its support. L.P. Loomis, the editor of the *Canadian Record*, penned an editorial after passage of the national amendment. "Well, the tallow dippers [old-fashioned thinkers] of Texas had the laugh on us the way they swamped Woman's Suffrage, but the National Congress came to our rescue and enacted a federal Woman' Suffrage law, and we who laugh last laugh best."

Texas became the ninth state and the first southern state to ratify on June 28, 1919. In August 1920, the Nineteenth Amendment became part of the Constitution.

THE 1906 MURDER THAT SHOCKED AMARILLO

Marty Kuhlman

On an afternoon in early October 1906, James Calvert, a thirteen-year-old boy, stumbled across a badly beaten man, naked and lying motionless along the railroad tracks. Calvert ran for help while Z.Z. Savage and others carried the barely conscious young man, no more than a teenager himself, to Dr. S.W. McMeans's office in downtown Amarillo.

Upon closer inspection, the doctor found that the unidentified teen had been struck in the face at least ten times with a hatchet. Although he mumbled some indistinct phrases, the teen never regained consciousness and succumbed to his wounds two days later.

City Marshal John Snider, who led a police force of three to patrol Amarillo's population of five thousand, went to work investigating the crime. After finding the victim's clothes in a railroad tank car under four feet of water, Snider placed them on the body, took a photograph and sent the photos to a number of out-of-town newspapers.

The young man was identified when W.H. Dockray of Amarillo saw the body and was struck by its resemblance to his brother, Silas. W.H. believed that the corpse might be that of his nephew Earl, so W.H. sent a photograph to his brother, who lived on a farm in Oklahoma Territory. Silas had been waiting two weeks for Earl's return and, after receiving the photo, caught the first train to Amarillo. The deceased was indeed his son.

Foster Earl Dockray was born in Blanco County, Texas, on October 13, 1888. He grew up on a farm outside Johnson City and, according to Amarillo's *Twice-a-Week Herald*, became accustomed to "hard work, temperate habits, and clean living." He attended the public school in Johnson City and gained a "good reputation throughout the entire community."

In May 1906, the eighteen-year-old joined a railroad construction camp in El Paso. Dockray traveled to construction camps all over West Texas, and by September, he was working as night watchmen at a camp in Hereford.

On October 3, Dockray wrote to his father that he was leaving Hereford for the farm. Earl reported that he had purchased a new suit of clothes and would bring home $120 (about $3,000 in 2017 dollars) that he had saved from his wages. Earl then left camp with his suitcase for Amarillo.

When citizens of Amarillo learned the identity and youth of the victim, the crime became "blacker and more foul." A number of people wrote cards or expressed sympathy to the Dockrays.

The businesses on Polk Street closed for Dockray's funeral, held at the Filmore Street Presbyterian Church. The service "was filled and overflowing with people from Amarillo who felt the pathos and the tragedy of the time," and a number of the city's gardens gave "their choicest treasures as tribute."

Reverend L.C. Kirkes declared in the service that the crime called the citizens to clean up "sections of this city" that were "positively unsafe." Amarillo's citizens raised a reward of $1,500 in less than three weeks after the murder. The reward eventually rose to $2,000 (equal to more than $50,000 in 2017 dollars).

Snider and detective W.A. Stewart of the Santa Fe Railroad circulated a description at railroad depots of the "cheap, greenish colored, imitation leather" suitcase Earl Dockray had carried. When Snider and Stewart discovered that a suitcase matching the description had been shipped to the depot in Wichita, Kansas, it led to the arrest of Frank Ellsworth.

Ellsworth had worked as a porter at DeWitt's saloon in Amarillo's Bowery District. The Bowery District—filled with saloons, brothels and gambling dens—had the reputation of hosting transients, gamblers, prostitutes and "thugs who would slug you for a quarter—or kill you for a dollar."

Ellsworth had met Dockray at a restaurant in Hereford and became intrigued when Dockray pulled out a "roll of greenbacks" to pay for cold drinks. They both then returned to Amarillo, where Dockray probably rented a room in the bowery, which was close to the train station.

In the trial of the *State of Texas v. Frank Ellsworth*, a number of witnesses testified that the suitcase Ellsworth had been found with was the same one

Amarillo's Bowery at an unknown date. The streets are still dirt, and a cow runs free in the neighborhood. A Route 66 marker stands in the center of the street. *Courtesy Marty Kuhlman.*

Dockray had owned, even identifying the ink stain made when Dockray had used it as a writing table. The jury found this and other circumstantial evidence enough to sentence Ellsworth to life in prison, although Ellsworth insisted that he was innocent. He was later paroled.

The murder shined a light on the city's small police force. When the city council met a week after the crime, a "full discussion of the means for enforcing all laws" was the main aspect of the agenda, and one solution was to add another officer.

The murder of Earl Dockray shocked Amarillo and forced the town to become more involved with law and order.

WEST TEXAS STATE RALLIES AROUND THE FLAG

Marty Kuhlman

When World War II broke out, the people of the United States rallied around the flag. Residents of the Llano Estacado did the same, and a small college in Canyon played an important role.

The War Department announced a program in late 1942 where thousands of young men would go to colleges across the nation to receive physical and academic preflight training. In January 1943, the commander of the U.S. Army Air Force sent President Joseph Hill of West Texas State Teachers College (WTSTC) a letter requesting that the air force be allowed to use the WT campus for training. Hill quickly agreed, and a few months later, the 350th Air Force College Training Detachment, consisting of approximately four hundred airmen, came to the campus.

There, the young airmen went through physical training, and they sang as they marched around campus. But the lyrics of one song contained the word *hell*, and according to then coed Merrie Duflot, "one sweet old lady" complained and the singing came to a halt. The ominous sound of silent marching took over.

Airmen also went to academic classes, where they were taught civil air regulations, geography, mathematics, health, physics and English. Generally, the cadet candidates did well in most classes but tended to put out less effort in English, as it was deemed "insignificant."

WEST TEXAS STATE AND THE WARS

This graphic from West Texas State's 1946 yearbook, *Le Mirage*, captures the spirit of the school's cooperation with the military during World War II. *Graphic courtesy University Archives Collection, Cornette Library, West Texas A&M University.*

The last phase of training included actual flying. Airmen flew ten small airplanes from an airfield north of Canyon, now the site of Frank Kimbrough Memorial Stadium. Each airman trained for forty-five minutes per day.

The training program lasted for five months and consisted of more than seven hundred hours. After graduation, the airmen became cadets and departed the campus for more training at established military bases, and another group of fresh candidates replaced them. During a two-year period, more than 1,800 cadets received training at WTSTC, and when the training detachment left the school in June 1944, the U.S. Army Air Force presented an award to the college recognizing its "superior services to the war effort."

But the appearance of the 350th also brought on other changes to the campus. At the beginning of the war, males accounted for one-third of the student body, but many left school to join the military. By 1944, male enrollment had fallen to 14 percent. Coeds were especially pleased to have such a large body of young military men on campus, and the airmen were excited to see coeds.

However, both the military and the college administration wanted to limit the fraternization between the prospective cadets and coeds. Captain D.L. Echols, the first commander of the 350th, laid down rules. For example, trainees could not acknowledge greetings from or enter into conversations with civilians and had a curfew at 2100 hours, or 9:00 p.m.

His replacement, Captain R.C. Corbyn, later loosened the rules and put the cadets on the honor code.

On weekends, the airmen met coeds for dances at the female dormitory, Cousins Hall, and for roller skating at Burton's Gym. But on weekdays, their free time was filled with sports, movies or studying.

But the natural attraction often proved too strong. Coeds and airmen clandestinely met on a tennis court between the barracks and Cousins Hall. One officer had the duty of searching the court each evening and shining a flashlight in the corners to break up any amorous activities. The searcher gained the title of the "Flashlight Packin' Major." At the time, the airmen knew a popular song to the tune of "Pistol Packin' Mama" which told the major to "lay that flashlight down." On at least one occasion, the flashlight disappeared.

The 350th even printed a newspaper, *Prop Dust*. The paper reported on promotions within the unit, but columns, cartoons and the occasional poem dealt mostly with relationships between airmen and coeds. The young men became so involved with coeds that the paper chose "a sweetheart of the week," and freshman Fern Cunningham became the sweetheart for the year in 1944. One column mentioned, "Proposals have been flying thick and fast this week." Some relationships became serious, as *Prop Dust* reported a number of marriages between airmen and coeds or Canyon residents.

WTSTC jumped at the chance to help the war effort, but the college was also aided by the 350th. The influx of student/soldiers meant job security for many instructors, who may have otherwise lost their jobs due to the declining enrollment during the war.

Almost all new construction ceased in Texas during the war, but the state did construct two buildings at state-supported colleges in 1942, and one of them was on the campus of WTSTC. The detachment even helped Canyon's economy, such as when airmen were taken en masse to get haircuts.

A small college in West Texas helped the war effort. Soldiers were trained, but other aspects of life changed as well.

INTEGRATION AT WEST TEXAS STATE COLLEGE

Marty Kuhlman

Before 1950, the vast majority of colleges in Texas were designated for Whites only. When West Texas State Normal College in Canyon opened its doors in 1910, the college offered an education to "any white person of good moral standing." At the time, the only state-supported college in the state for African Americans was Prairie View A&M at Prairie View, near Houston.

Some movement toward desegregation of higher education appeared in the Panhandle when Amarillo's chapter of the National Association for the Advancement of Colored People (NAACP) argued that Black residents paid city taxes, which supported Amarillo College (AC), and had a right to attend. AC admitted four Black students in 1951 and became one of the first colleges in the state to integrate.

In 1954, the Supreme Court ended the doctrine of "separate but equal" in public education with the *Brown v. Board of Education of Topeka, Kansas* case. But Texas, like the rest of the South, held on to segregation as long as possible.

West Texas State College (WTSC), located in White and conservative Canyon, did not help the chances of desegregation. The community, like most in West Texas at the time, was a "sundown town," where Black folks were not allowed to be in town after nightfall. Even the famous ranch historian J. Evetts Haley was an ardent segregationist, as well as being a prominent and influential citizen of Canyon. He ran for governor 1956 touting a segregation platform. When a federal court ordered the University of Texas system to desegregate at the undergraduate level in the mid-1950s, an editorial in the *Canyon News* lamented the decision and stated, "We are happy, indeed, that Canyon does not have a Negro population."

Soon after, Guy Raleigh Tomlin—a fifty-seven-year-old instructor at the Amarillo Air Force Base who had taught in Amarillo's Black schools and been principal of Frederick Douglass Elementary and Patten High School—became the first African American to apply for entry into WTSTC. Tomlin hoped to take classes in education needed for a higher teaching position at the base. He was not allowed to enter the school.

Then, in 1959, twenty-one-year-old John Matthew Shipp Jr.—a graduate of Amarillo's George Washington Carver High School and Amarillo College and an employee of the Amarillo Air Force Base—applied for admission, seeking to further his career. WTSC turned him down on two separate occasions.

The NAACP had been outlawed in Texas when Tomlin had applied, but by 1959, the group was again legal and came to Shipp's aid. W.J. Durham, the principal lawyer for the Texas chapter, brought a case in the U.S. District Court in Amarillo. Durham argued that WTSC only allowed White students to enroll while utilizing public funds and had violated Shipp's "rights secured to him under the Fourteenth Amendment." But the segregationist-leaning state government of Texas helped WTSC fight to remain for Whites only and sent the state's assistant attorney general, Henry G. Braswell, to represent the college in court.

The defense team admitted that Shipp had been rejected solely on race but claimed that since some colleges in the state had desegregated, such as Midwestern University and North Texas State College, others did not need to. The defense adopted what the state's attorney general in 1956, John Ben Sheppard, had called the "salt-and-pepper plan." Sheppard announced that some people would accept salt and pepper mixed together, or integration. But others wanted salt only, or all-White institutions, while others wanted pepper only, or all-Black schools.

In February 1960, federal judge Joe B. Dooley found the state's argument to maintain exclusionary colleges to be unconstitutional and ordered WTSC to admit Shipp. But Shipp, having already lost considerable time trying to be enrolled, went to college elsewhere and graduated with a Bachelor of Science degree from the University of Houston.

Mae Deane Franklin and Roy Wilkins were among the first African Americans to attend West Texas State after the school was integrated in the early 1960s. *Courtesy University Archives Collection, Cornette Library, West Texas A&M University.*

Although Shipp did not attend, Judge Dooley's decision had a tremendous impact. One day after the decision, the *Amarillo Daily News* reported that the judgment "rattled the doors of all other Texas state supported schools."

Integration came to Texas Tech University in 1961 (Haley leaving the board of regents of Tech helped the chances for integration), the University of Houston in 1962 and Texas A&M University in 1963.

Betty Jo Thomas of Wichita Falls became the first African American student to attend WTSC in the fall of 1960. She attended WT through 1964 but did not graduate. Helen Neal had moved to Amarillo in 1955 and brought college credit from the all-Black Langston College in Oklahoma. She could not finish her education after moving, however, as there was not a close four-year college she could attend. Finally, the desegregation of WTSC, only twenty miles to the south, became an opportunity. Neal enrolled in the spring of 1961 and became the college's first African American graduate in August 1962.

Like the rest of the state, much of the Panhandle and West Texas had dragged its feet, but the federal court in Amarillo brought desegregation to WTSC, which influenced the rest of Texas.

PART VII

LASTING IMPRESSIONS

A football stadium, a park and several buildings at Texas Tech bear the names of individuals who had a profound influence on the development of the university in its early years. Jones Stadium honors Clifford B. Jones, who played a leading role in the creation and the design of Texas Tech and later became its president, even though he had no college degree.

Two buildings honor early faculty members, W.L. Stangel and W. C. Holden, whose influence led to the development of the university's outstanding agricultural and museum programs. And a beautiful little park on the southwest side of the campus is named for Elo Urbanovsky, whose vision led Tech to becoming one of the most beautiful landscaped campuses in the nation.

Also, in north Lubbock, a now closed Minnie Tubbs Elementary School building memorializes the community's first teacher. While not memorialized, there is another name in Lubbock's history that deserves remembering, and this chapter helps to do that by recounting the story of one of the most outstanding football players who ever played in Jones Stadium, Gabriel "Señor Sack" Rivera.

MISS MINNIE TUBBS

LUBBOCK'S FIRST TEACHER

Jack Becker

L ubbock's first school opened its doors in the fall of 1891, eighteen years before Lubbock became an incorporated town. Also that fall, Lubbock's jail opened, and the first school was held in the jail!

Holding school in the jail was not a reflection on Lubbock's schoolchildren. Its first school building was still under construction, and after one semester at the jail, Lubbock's students moved to the new schoolhouse; some remember it for being "nice" because it had wooden floors.

The area's first teacher was a determined young sixteen-year-old woman by the name of Minnie Tubbs. A member of one of the pioneering families of Lubbock, Minnie, as described by her friends, was smart, pretty and very mature for her age. For example, even before Lubbock organized a school system, Minnie created a subscription-based school where parents paid her to teach their children.

Twenty-five children enrolled for classes that first year, but only about half attended on any given day. And half of the children, who made up grades one through seven, were related to Minnie, including her own sister, Anne. Others were her cousins, the children of her aunt and uncle Isham and Texana Tubbs. Uncle Isham was on the Lubbock County School Board when Minnie became Lubbock's first teacher.

The first school year started in mid-April 1891 and ended early in June 1892. The children found the jail and school sparsely furnished by today's standards. The jail had a dirt floor, but most children sat on wooden benches furnished by parents and read from well-worn textbooks. The children wrote their lessons on slate boards.

Minnie taught every subject and every grade, offering not only the standard reading, writing and arithmetic but also geography, civics and penmanship. She also knew how to handle children, as she could, by today's standards, distribute tough punishment if students did not know their lessons or acted up in class. She spanked children if they misbehaved and even made her own sister sit in the corner with a dunce cap on her head when she failed to live up to Minnie's high standards.

The younger students attended school until noon, but the older ones in grades five through seven stayed the entire day. After school, Minnie remained until 5:30 p.m. preparing the next day's lessons. Her salary was a reported $32.50 per month.

Although a strict but fair disciplinarian, Minnie had to deal with the first student-led walkout to take place in a Lubbock school. On April 1, 1892, Aprils Fool's Day, every student walked out—or, more correctly, ran away from school, planning to spend the day playing down in Yellow House Canyon. Minnie caught sight of them just as they disappeared down the canyon. The children expected some pretty harsh punishment for their act of rebellion but were obviously willing to suffer the consequences.

When the children stopped running long enough to look back, they saw Minnie walking slowly toward them. In her hand they saw not a switch but a bag. As Minnie got closer, the children noticed that she did not seem the least bit upset. When she got close enough to talk to the children, she asked them to sit with her on some nearby rocks.

Minnie then distributed the contents of the bag she was carrying, stick candy, and then joined the twelve "escapees" in a day of fun—playing games, relaxing and talking. This may have been the first, but it was not the last time Lubbock students left school on April Fool's Day. Obviously, Minnie was a wise beyond her years, an excellent teacher and a master of the use of reverse psychology.

Minnie remained in Lubbock only one year and then moved to Crosby County and taught the 1892–93 school year in Emma, which was at the time a bigger town than Lubbock. While there she met and married Van Sanders, a local cowboy, on June 13, 1893. Many of her cousins remember taking the long wagon trip to Emma to see their older cousin and favorite teacher get married. They remembered traveling late into the night and falling asleep on the bed of the wagon.

Minnie Tubbs with her husband, Van Sanders, shortly after their marriage in 1893. *Courtesy Southwest Collection, Texas Tech University.*

Tragically Minnie died young, soon after giving birth to her son, Sylvan, on June 1, 1894—barely a year married and only nineteen years of age. In later years, both she and her uncle, Isham, were memorialized with the naming of Tubbs Elementary School (1964–2012), located on the 3300 block of Bates Avenue, in their honor.

CLIFFORD B. JONES

"WEST TEXAS NO. I CITIZEN"

Jennifer Spurrier

C lifford Bartlett Jones was born on April 9, 1886, in Rico, Colorado. He died on November 27, 1972. Between his birth and death, he earned the nickname "West Texas No. 1 Citizen" and witnessed having a major college football stadium named in his honor.

Just what did Jones do to earn this to earn such distinction? The answer is chronicled in various resources housed at the Southwest Collection at Texas Tech University in ranch records, his papers, records of Texas Tech and through oral interviews.

Before moving to West Texas, Jones lived in Missouri, where he engaged in business. His father, Charles A. Jones, moved to Dickens County to become manager of the S.M. Swenson Spur Ranch in 1907, and four years later, he hired Clifford to become his assistant. In 1913, the elder Jones moved to manage other Swenson properties, but Clifford remained and helped to establish the town of Spur.

But Jones wasn't your average cowboy. He became involved in banking and served on several bank boards throughout his life. He served as a civic leader throughout the region, including being mayor of Spur, a founder and president of the West Texas Chamber of Commerce, a 33rd degree Mason, a director for the Scottish Rite Foundation of Texas and a regional advisor for the Public Works Administration in Texas.

In Lubbock, Jones is remembered for his long affiliation with Texas Tech. As a founder of the West Texas Chamber of Commerce, he was heavily involved in the early 1920s effort to get a state college in West Texas. In 1923, when Texas Tech became that fulfillment, Jones was appointed to its first board of directors, and in 1925, he became chairman of the board. His vision and direction helped to mold the new school.

In 1939, Jones became the third president of Texas Tech, but the appointment was not without controversy. Jones had no academic credentials—he had not attended an institute of higher education and had no degrees, except for a high school education. Moreover, at the time of his appointment, he was still serving as chairman of the board of directors for the college. Regional papers reported on the unfolding drama, but Jones's candidacy—he had been named as "West Texas No. 1 Citizen" by the press as early as 1925—was widely supported.

As president, Jones accomplished several goals in spite of the difficult war years. He established the Texas Tech Foundation and helped increase student housing, which helped Tech become the state's third-largest school. He was a much-respected administrator during his tenure; his business sensibilities and his strong leadership overshadowed his lack of formal higher education. Jones served as president from 1939 until 1944, when he retired due to purported health issues. The board then named him President Emeritus, a position he took seriously and would hold until his death.

After Jones resigned, he continued to be active, both in his business endeavors and in his support of Texas Tech. Jones and his wife contributed $100,000 to help fund a football stadium for the college, and the Clifford B. and Audrey Jones Stadium opened in 1947, with the first game played there in November in front of a full house of twenty-seven thousand fans. They continued to support Tech with other gifts. In time, after receiving several honorary degrees, he become known as Dr. Jones.

In 1968, at a Masonic banquet in Lubbock, newspaper editor Charley Guy introduced Jones. Guy offered that Jones obtained his nickname, "West Texas No. 1 Citizen," in the early 1930s, when Max Bentley, the managing editor of the *Abilene Reporter-News*, wrote that Jones should be the next congressman from the area because he was "West Texas No. 1 Citizen." Guy also noted that "Clifford Jones began his adult career as little more than a boy with a small firm in Kansas City. Through application of his mind, his talents and his industry, he became important in many areas and to many people."

As Texas Tech president, Clifford B. Jones, *right*, confers with Texas governor Coke Stevenson, who served from 1941 to 1947. *Courtesy Southwest Collection, Texas Tech University.*

When Clifford B. Jones died in 1972, the *Lubbock Avalanche-Journal* ran an article titled "West Texas Loses 'First Citizen.'" The article noted, "There is not a person driving the highways, attending Texas Tech, associated in civic undertakings, working for a livelihood in West Texas today who is not in some way better for having had Clifford Bartlett Jones as a friend or a neighbor." While many have contributed to this region, the efforts of Jones—a cowboy, a banker, an educator and a true service-oriented man—will long be remembered.

THE LASTING IMPRESSION OF W.L. STANGEL

Jennifer Spurrier

When Texas Technological College was born in 1923, several of its first faculty played key roles in shaping the institution. One that especially influenced the school was the W.L. Stangel of the School of Agriculture.

The Southwest Collection at Texas Tech University holds his papers and several oral history interviews with him. Among his papers are documents related to his time at Texas Tech, his development of livestock judging activities and personal materials related to his civic activities.

Wenzel Louis Stangel was born in 1889 to John and Ann Stangel in Stangelville, Wisconsin, which was named after his family. His mother died when he was three. His father remarried, and soon after, in the late 1890s, the family moved to Texas.

Stangel was considered short in height. He was given the nickname "Runt," and he would keep this nickname throughout his life. But he would eventually get other names of distinction, such as "Mr. Southwest Agriculture."

He attended Fort Worth's North Side High School, where he was the captain of its first football team. After graduation in 1910, he attended Texas A&M. In 1915, he graduated with a Bachelor of Science degree in animal husbandry. The following year, he went to the University of Missouri, where he earned a master's degree in 1916. Stangel then returned

W.L. Stangel as a young professor when he first arrived at Texas Technological College, circa 1930. *Courtesy Southwest Collection, Texas Tech University.*

to Texas A&M, where he was hired to teach animal husbandry and coach the livestock judging team. In 1919, the team won the international collegiate judging competition in Chicago. With such success, Stangel was soon appointed full professor.

In December 1920, Stangel married Mary Ruth Canon, and five years later, he joined the first faculty at the new Texas Technological College and moved to Lubbock. The Stangels would have two daughters: Mary Menon, born in 1923, and Ava Ruth, who was born in 1925 as the first faculty baby at Texas Tech. Both daughters would go on to graduate from Texas Tech.

When Tech opened for classes in the fall of 1925, the School of Agriculture was under the direction of Arthur H. Leidigh, who was the one who hired Stangel and Charles H. Mahoney as his first two faculty members. Stangel would teach animal husbandry and Mahoney horticulture.

Leidigh himself taught classes in agronomy. Upon opening, the only agriculture buildings were the Dairy Barn (not completed) and the Livestock Pavilion. Stangel had selected the location of the Dairy Barn and assisted the architect with its design. It became a very functional building, one that suited the needs of the animal husbandry program.

In that first fall of 1925, Stangel offered three courses. On just the second day of classes, according to an interview he gave in 1973, Stangel took his students to see a sick cow he had located in someone's backyard. He used the Hereford to instruct students on all of the animal's shortcomings.

With limited funds, the Department of Agriculture faculty had to be resourceful. Leidigh, Stangel and Mahoney obtained donations of livestock and machinery to help get the school's needed resources. Before long, they were able to start a college dairy herd, and students were allowed to bring their own cows for use in the program; in turn, they could earn funds for college by selling milk. According to the Texas Technological College October 1925 *Bulletin*, a student was limited to three cows.

As the years passed, Stangel continued teaching animal husbandry courses, encouraging the growth of the school, coaching livestock judging teams, and taking an active role in athletics by serving on the athletics committee (he would be on the committee for twenty-five years).

In addition, he actively participated in livestock events throughout Texas and the nation at venues such as the State Fair and the Fort Worth Livestock Show, serving in various capacities such as judge, superintendent and show manager. He became well known as a knowledgeable and competent judge and administrator.

When Dean Leidigh retired in 1945, Stangel was appointed dean of the School of Agriculture, a position he held until retirement in 1958. When he retired, the *Lubbock Avalanche-Journal* announced the event with his headline, "West Texas' Favorite Dean Retires."

Dean Stangel served Texas Tech for a total of thirty-three years, and upon his retirement, he was named Dean Emeritus. At a portrait presentation of Stangel in 1956, one former student offered that Stangel was a "great, modest, humble man" who "cared about the general welfare of students." Stangel died in 1978, but he is still remembered on the Tech campus. A residence hall bears his name, and in the College of Agricultural Sciences and Natural Resources, there is an endowed scholarship that honors him as well.

W.C. HOLDEN AND THE EARLY DEVELOPMENT OF THE MUSEUM AT TEXAS TECH UNIVERSITY

Cameron L. Saffell

As early as October 1925, writers in the new Texas Tech newspaper, *The Toreador*, wrote of the need for a museum. A 1928 editorial said, "It would be a good idea for Texas Tech to begin the collection of items which would be of untold interest to future generations." One campus member who had an interest was Mary Woodward Doak, Dean of Women and professor of English. In the summer of 1928, Doak participated in a summer vacation course to England that included a visit to the British Museum, a virtual encyclopedia of research and entertainment about the material culture of the British empire.

What Doak saw melded with the ideas for a museum expressed by other faculty members, including history and sociology professor Dr. John Granbery, who suggested a committee organize to establish the same kind of museum at Texas Technological College. On March 27, 1929, a small group of Tech's faculty and students met to form a "museum society" and help departments to collect objects and display them. By its second meeting on May 2, the group was calling itself the Plains Museum Society, now drawing interested people from throughout West Texas and Eastern New Mexico. Its stated mission was to "foster, increase and diffuse knowledge and appreciation of the sciences and to encourage collections and the study of scientific, historic, and artifact value in a museum."

Over the summer, a diverse collection of initial donations was assembled: prehistoric Indian tools, items of ranch life, tools from Fort Griffin and Fort Phantom Hill and archaeological evidence of Plains Indians tribes. To help oversee the collection, Granbery recruited in 1929 an "experienced" museum person to join the Tech faculty. W.C. Holden of McMurry College had started a museum there two years earlier to keep students out of mischief. With his history and anthropology background, this was enough to hire him as a professor and name him the society's second curator.

As early as 1931, the Plains Museum Society informally talked about creating a permanent and dedicated museum building, but nothing came of it until 1935. That year, the society's annual program pointed at a specific mission: "West Texans should preserve physical evidence of the past" of the region.

Its supporters, after learning that the Texas legislature was appropriating $3 million to celebrate the upcoming 1936 centennial of Texas independence, began to lobby for funds for a museum, but they learned that state planners had only recommended giving Lubbock $14,000 for a bronze statue honoring Thomas Lubbock. The society rallied support and mobilized to appeal to the full Centennial Commission for a museum instead.

Holden and others rallied support from sixty-seven West Texas counties—turning out residents from as far away as Tulia, Sweetwater, Odessa, Muleshoe, Ozona, Big Spring and Mason—to convoy to Austin to personally appear before the commission. On October 20, 1935, their appeal yielded a small victory, as the *Lubbock Avalanche-Journal* announced the allocation of $25,000 for a museum at Texas Tech—not enough to complete a building but enough to get started.

In February 1936, the Plains Museum Society gathered for its seventh annual meeting with a key proposal on the agenda: changing the group's name. Citing the previous year's campaigns and the informal work of individuals from throughout the region, officers felt that it important to recognize the efforts. "We are anxious to keep this group held in a close-knit organization. Therefore it appears to our advantage to change our name... to that of the West Texas Museum Association."

Campus and local officials joined members of the West Texas Museum Association on September 23, 1936, to break ground for the new building. With the small state appropriation, everyone agreed that they would build the basement level first. A grand staircase led up to a flat concrete slab four feet above the surrounding land. Only a small sign indicated what it was, with an arrow pointing down the interior stairway entrance. It quickly became a popular joke among students, particularly when writing home asking for money or trying to reconcile with their sweetheart, that if the respondent did not comply the writer would "jump off the museum."

In 1940, the museum launched the Give a Brick campaign and financial drives to raise $226,000 ($2.3 million, adjusted for inflation) to finish the building. The project was delayed by World War II but completed in 1949, when the upper two stories and the rotunda were built on top of the basement level completed thirteen years earlier.

William Curry Holden, circa 1944. *Courtesy Texas State Historical Association.*

Upon its completion, Texas Tech and the museum association recognized Holden's longtime leadership role and changed his job title from curator to being the first director of the museum. That year, Holden said that the museum "should be a place which would make people proudly conscious as a rich past upon which a vivid present and fruitful future can be built."

Three years later, the West Texas Museum Association announced the purchase of a Spitz planetarium, which opened in a small adobe building outside, as well as the commissioning of southwestern artist Peter Hurd to create a mural for the Rotunda's Memorial Hall profiling South Plains pioneers. By the mid-1950s, the museum was easily the most popular attraction in Lubbock.

ELO J. URBANOVSKY

EARLY ARCHITECT OF THE TTU CAMPUS

Lynn Whitfield

T he TTU campus is very much a walking campus, highlighted by striking Spanish renaissance architecture and a nationally recognized public art collection that includes numerous outdoor sculptures and attractive landscaping. Over the years, the landscaping has evolved to become more water efficient and climate friendly. It certainly wasn't this way in 1949, when Elo J. Urbanovsky accepted a teaching position in Lubbock.

As Tech's early landscape architect, Urbanovsky faced a challenging task in addressing infrastructure shortfalls such as lack of sidewalks, streets in need of paving, overcrowded parking lots and limited funding to throw at these problems. Urbanovsky wanted to pair the college with the city but was determined to maintain the school's separate identity and the integrity of a unified landscape. His initial focus was on the center part of the campus, later known as the Historic District of Texas Tech.

Positioning the new Will Rogers statue was one of his first planning projects. Early suggestions of placing the statue at the Broadway entrance were overridden because the horse's rear would face east, thus mooning downtown supporters. With a chuckle, Urbanovsky later recalled that the statue's final location was moved closer to Memorial Circle and that the horse's rear oriented to face a different direction: toward Texas A&M!

Urbanovsky was born in the town of West, Texas, on December 20, 1907, and was a 1931 graduate of Texas A&M. His diverse work experiences prior to Tech included teaching in the San Antonio school system, serving as regional landscape architect for the U.S. Department of Agriculture and teaching at his alma mater at College Station.

He answered his country's call to duty during World War II, serving in the U.S. Navy. Later, from 1949 to 1975, he helped coordinate and synchronize the complex development of all new facilities and roadways at Tech, concurrently seeking to balance a beautification program with a design to maintain the feeling of wide-open country so inherently a part of West Texas. The Department of Park Administration and Landscape Architecture was established under his leadership.

He was not without his critics. He was described as stubborn and slow in his

Elo J. Urbanovsky, whose vision for the Texas Tech transformed it into one of the nation's most beautiful campuses. *Courtesy University Archives, Southwest Collection, Texas Tech University.*

deliberations when plotting out the school's many landscape and traffic expansions. The "Prof," as he was known to his eager-to-please students, was tough and demanding. Urbanovsky expected his students to be driven, polished and well versed in the audiovisual technology of the day. Dr. Pat Taylor, former director of landscape architecture at the University of Texas at Arlington, remarked of his mentor, "He insisted that showmanship be matched with substance." Those who knew him well added that underneath his crusty demeanor lay a "a real softie."

The Prof's passion for beautifying the state and supporting its network of historic sites and parks caught the attention of some very illustrious admirers. Governor John Connally chose him to serve in 1967 on the state committee focused on creating a "Travel Trails of Texas" program.

Soon afterward, the Coordinating Board of the State of Texas approved federal funding for a multi-institution pilot program surveying Dallas parks, to be headed by Urbanovsky. Meanwhile, First Lady of the United States Lady Bird Johnson sought out his acquaintance, thus leading to a long collaboration between the two. He served on her beautification committee for a decade, working on different projects, including the enhancement of the LBJ Ranch. Later, he was chosen to serve on a state advisory committee, which planned the development of the Lyndon B. Johnson State Park.

Governor Preston Smith, in 1970, appointed him to serve on the newly created Texas Conservation Foundation.

On the Tech campus, the early 1970s brought some grief to the assiduous planner. Delays in financing a new Recreation Center, controversy about a campus loop under development and complaints about the lack of parking were all editorialized in the student newspaper. All these reflected some of the many growing pains for a college transitioning into a university of international prominence under the guidance of a new president, Grover E. Murray.

Through it all, Urbanovsky stuck to his ideals of the campus being attractively landscaped, with well-placed pathways laid out to encourage pedestrian mobility. His highly distinguished career was filled with professional awards and accolades, such as being named an early Horn Professor and a recipient of the *Pro Excelsia et Pontifice* by Pope John XXIII. In 1978, Urbanovsky and his wife, Olga, established an endowed fellowship, funded with a $75,000 matching grant from friend Laurence Rockefeller. The fellowship provided financial assistance for a TTU graduate students studying land use, planning or management.

Following his passing in 1988, Kenneth May, *Lubbock Avalanche-Journal* writer and longtime friend, publicly acknowledged Elo's "jealous guarding of every inch of university property," concluding that "for so long as there is a Texas Tech University campus sprouting trees and shrubbery in an eye-appealing landscape, he will be immortal."

The university honored the late visionary on October 1, 1993, with the dedication of the pedestrian-friendly Urbanovsky Park.

GABE RIVERA

SEÑOR SACK OF TEXAS TECH FOOTBALL

Jorge Iber

Over their history, like most large football programs, the Texas Tech University Red Raiders have had many great players, with a total of eleven individuals garnering selection as consensus first-team All-Americans. An even more select few have merited both All-American status as well as induction into the College Football Hall of Fame. Among these legends of the Lubbock gridiron are the great E.J. Holub (inducted in 1986), Donny Anderson (1989), Dave Parks (2008) and Zach Thomas (2015).

The subject of this essay, Gabriel Rivera, is another member of this august company. His legend, which would grow exponentially during his time in Lubbock, started to blossom in San Antonio and eventually generated national attention (for both positive and negative reasons) in the early 1980s. There were four key moments in Gabe's athletic and personal life that helped shape his story.

First, Rivera, who was born in Crystal City, began to gain notoriety as a two-way player (as a tight end and linebacker) for the Jefferson High School Mustangs in San Antonio. He made All-City as a junior after the 1977 season and followed that honor with selection to the nationally prestigious Parade All-American team, winning the Thom McAn Award (given to the best player in the San Antonio area) after the 1978 campaign.

Needless to say, this recognition made Gabe a highly sought-after commodity among a plethora of collegiate recruiters. One local paper

Gabriel "Gabe" Rivera during his senior year in 1982. *Courtesy Texas Tech Athletics.*

estimated the number of potential suitors at as many as fifteen, including the fabled Notre Dame Fighting Irish. Among the institutions that he planned to visit were Arizona, Baylor, Texas Tech and up to three more schools. By early February 1979, Gabe had made his (surprising) choice: he would become a Red Raider.

Upon his arrival on campus in the late summer of that year, he began a meteoric rise that would bring him to the pinnacle of the football world: selection as a first-round draft choice in the National Football League draft.

The second key moment is this: while there were many games in which Rivera starred, one in the 1982 season stood out clearly from the rest. Over the decades, the eyes of all of collegiate football have not often focused intently on the Red Raiders, but the team certainly was in the national spotlight on October 23, 1982. On that day, Tech played in Seattle against the then number one–ranked University of Washington (a team that would finish ranked seventh that year).

First, though, a little background. Any aficionado of collegiate football can almost instinctually rattle off the names of the sport's most historically "elite" and "celebrated" programs. When discussing any chronicle of the game, it is fair to say that teams such as the Alabama Crimson Tide, Notre Dame Fighting Irish, Ohio State Buckeyes, Texas Longhorns (painful though it may be to admit), Oklahoma Sooners and the Michigan Wolverines stand out from the vast majority of institutions that field programs in the highest echelons of gridiron competition.

The Red Raiders have had memorable years, claiming (as of the end of the 2018 season) a total of a dozen conference titles or co-championships. Nine of these came while in the Border Conference (which Tech was a part of between 1932 and 1956), two during their time in the Southwest Conference (which Tech was a part of between 1957 and 1996) and one South Division co-title in the Big XII (which Tech has been a member of since 1996). The school's squads have played in a total of thirty-eight bowl games, including the Cotton Bowl on four occasions (all defeats), with an overall mark of 13-24-1 in postseason competition.

Going into this 1982 contest against Washington, the Raiders sported a mediocre 3-3 record, with victories over Air Force, Texas A&M and Rice to go along with defeats suffered at the hands of New Mexico, Baylor and Arkansas. The Huskies, conversely, came in undefeated at 6-0 with impressive triumphs over Pac10 foes such as Arizona, Oregon, California and Oregon State. Not surprisingly, pigskin prognosticators forecast that the home team would steamroll the visitors from Lubbock.

For Washington, this contest was supposed to be but a midseason tune-up with an also-ran before the mighty Purple and Gold moved on to play highly ranked teams from UCLA and Arizona State later in the conference schedule. The Huskies came into the contest averaging more than forty points per game; a freakishly high total in the pre–air raid offensive era so common now in college football. Texas Tech, it was understood, had little chance.

On that autumn afternoon, however, something totally unforeseen occurred as the team at the top of the polls barely survived an unexpectedly stern challenge by the upstarts from western Texas. The final score of 10–3 in favor of Washington was so surprising that the Huskies actually dropped out of the top spot in the national polls post-contest.

After the final whistle, all that the national, Washington State and Lubbock media could talk about was not the Huskies' nail-biting triumph, but rather how one Tech player on the defensive side of the ball—a six-foot-two, 285-pound behemoth—had totally dominated the action on the field. Norval Pollard, Texas Tech football beat writer for the *Lubbock Avalanche-Journal*, summarized the stupendous play of no. 69 that day in the following manner:

> *Gabe was like a mad hornet trapped in a fast-moving car with all the windows up. The Huskies didn't know whether to pull over, open all the doors, and wait until he escaped or keep traveling and hope he stayed at the rear window. [Washington coach Don] James and his players lauded Rivera following the contest, and rightfully so. James, who rushed out to midfield after the game to congratulate Gabe, called him everything from "Superman" to the "best defensive player I've seen."*

The fuss was something to see and hear, but the greatest tribute to Gabe's play came Sunday morning in the two Seattle newspapers, the *Times* and

No. 69 Gabe Rivera blocks a pass in action against SMU in 1982. *Courtesy Texas Tech Athletics.*

the *Post-Intelligencer*. "Seldom, if ever, will you see a victory by the top team in the country—in its own stadium no less—upstaged by the play of one individual, especially a defensive player for the opposition, especially when the opposition happens to be non-conference from 1500 miles away." But Gabe couldn't be ignored.

It was performances such as this that brought Gabe to the attention of several NFL teams and a plethora of agents who sought to make him their client. Additionally, with the advent of the USFL in the early 1980s, athletes such as Rivera were even more sought-after and were in an even stronger bargaining position. The sky, it appeared, was the limit.

A third key moment in Gabe's life came as the various NFL franchises called out the names of their first-round selections in April 1983. Soon, attention focused on the Pittsburgh Steelers as they moved up to call out the twenty-first choice. At this time, the most dominant team of the 1970s was approaching a transitional phase. Among their needs were several concerns: Who would (eventually) replace Terry Bradshaw under center? Who would be the next outside threat to supplant the legendary Lynn Swann? Should they look to shore up the other side of the ball and begin to work at refortifying the fabled "Steel Curtain"? Did this draft class possibly contain someone who could be slotted to succeed another Texas legend, "Mean" Joe Greene? Pittsburgh's brain trust, the Rooney family and Coach Chuck Noll, decided to go with Rivera as their choice in the first round of the 1983 draft, eschewing another possibility: the selection of native son Dan Marino (who would, instead, go on to have a Hall of Fame career with the Miami Dolphins). Gabe signed a multi-year contract with the Steelers in May. He was now on his way to becoming a star and a millionaire! The future seemed very bright indeed.

The fourth key moment took place when all of these hopes, dreams and aspirations came crashing down in late October of that same year. After finishing practice, Gabe went to a restaurant for dinner and had a few beers with his meal. Later that evening, as he was driving his newly purchased Datsun 280ZX, Rivera had a violent collision with another vehicle and was ejected through the rear window of his sports car. For several days, he hovered close to death. He survived, but his spine was broken at T5-6, paralyzing him from the chest down. He would remain a paraplegic for the rest of his life. The fans in Western Pennsylvania, although greatly supportive, eventually came to refer to this former Red Raider great as "the Steeler that Never Was."

Beyond tragedy, several factors make Rivera's story distinctive. Not many Latinos (Mexican American in Gabe's case) were playing at the highest levels of collegiate football in the late 1970s and early 1980s; indeed, they still were not represented in substantial numbers even in the late 2010s. Yet Gabe came from a family who had seized on both education and football as mechanisms to carve out a middle-class life in 1950s segregated Texas. Indeed, Juan Rivera, Gabe's father, who also played football and graduated from Crystal City High School (in 1948), went on to play collegiately (at Howard Payne College, now Howard Payne University in Brownwood), earned two degrees (in education) and finally coached football and track in various communities in southern parts of the Lone Star State. Gabe would be among the select few athletes to move on from playing Division I football to the NFL.

Although the devastating accident would render his career among the shortest in NFL history, a mere six games, he would fight to overcome the physical and emotional trauma of this catastrophic event no less valiantly than he'd fought on the football field. Although there were many difficult years, Gabe eventually summoned the diligence and wherewithal to give back to his adopted homes of Lubbock and San Antonio and became a highly respected and beloved community figure.

On July 17, 2018, aficionados of the Texas Tech's football program awoke to learn of the passing of Gabriel Rivera. To those who followed the fortunes of the Red Raiders over the years, this giant of man was more widely and affectionately referred to as "Señor Sack." He was a shining star over the years of 1979–82 for a series of teams that finished with a combined mark of 13-28-3, with their best season being a mediocre 5-6 in 1980. The 1982 game versus the Washington Huskies was just one of Señor Sack's many memorable performances. According to his web page on the College Football Hall of Fame website (he was inducted in 2012), Rivera was a consensus All-American after the 1982 season. Further, he was honorable-mention All-American in 1980 and 1981 and earned first-team All–Southwest Conference honors his senior year.

Another legendary figure of Tech football, Rodney Allison, who is now the director of the lettermen's association (known as the Double T Varsity Club) and who interacted with Gabe and his family constantly in recent years, recalled one particular play that showcased and exemplified Rivera's truly unique skill set. In a contest against Arkansas, the Razorback quarterback (running an option play) broke through the Red Raiders' line into the open field. He continued to run toward Tech's goal line, only to be caught, from behind, almost sixty yards beyond the line of scrimmage by a lineman. Plays like these are what attracted and held the attention of the NFL and the nation.

PART VIII

THE GARDEN OF EDEN

At times, observers often see the Llano Estacado as a great garden, especially when cotton is in full bloom and corn and grain sorghum are turning ripe and ready for harvest. But it has also been proven to be a fertile field for artists and writers who see beyond the flat plains and often dusty sky.

This chapter tells of two regional artists whose work has been exhibited throughout the nation and recognizes the work of a Lubbock gardener who also brought national attention to a little purple flower. It also notes how the little town of Slaton became a personal Garden of Eden for a young boy who grew up on a Llano Estacado farm, as well as how the Southwest Collection at Texas Tech became a rich resource for historical research.

But it begins with recalling a very special time, when music flowered across the Texas Tech campus and John Philip Sousa came to town.

THE DAY JOHN PHILIP SOUSA CAME TO TOWN

Elissa Stroman

Passing by the south side of Texas Tech University's Administration building, you might miss a small sign near the parking lot. Added in 2005, it is a memorial to John Philip Sousa, who conducted his band in Lubbock on November 15, 1928. Sousa's appearance on the Llano Estacado is a somewhat forgotten footnote of Lubbock musical history, but his connections to this region have become urban legends, often leading to more questions than answers.

Sousa's five-month tour across America in 1928 was part of his Golden Jubilee—his thirty-sixth annual tour and fiftieth anniversary as a conductor. In the weeks prior to his appearance in Lubbock, Sousa's seventy-six-piece ensemble performed across Oklahoma, Texas and New Mexico. His train arrived in town from Amarillo and the next day traveled to Brownwood. The Lubbock concerts took place at 3:00 p.m. and again at 8:15 p.m. in the Texas Tech gymnasium, also known as the "Old Mule Barn" (once located near today's football practice fields). The estimated total attendance for both concerts was between five and six thousand.

The Lubbock programs highlighted diverse works and instrumentation: a flute sextette, saxophone octette and soprano and xylophone solo features, along with longer programmatic work like Sousa's three-movement "Tales of a Traveler" and his band arrangement of Richard Strauss's "Death and Transfiguration." Sousa's best-known works—"El Capitan,"

John Philip

SOUSA

His Band!!

The World's Greatest Musical Organization

Two Performances

3 P. M. Matinee and High School
Band Concert | 8:15 P. M. Evening Concert

Thursday Nov. 15

AT THE

TEXAS TECH

EVERY SEAT RESERVED
at popular prices for both performances
AFTERNOON PRICES: 75c and $1.10
EVENING PRICES: $1 and $2
Seats now on sale at

BOWEN'S DRUG STORE
CITY DRUG STORES

MAIL AND TELEGRAPH ORDERS

promptly filled upon receipt of check. Address all
communications to the Business Office, Texas Tech
College.

Newspaper announcement of John Philip Sousa's appearance in the *Lubbock Morning Avalanche*, dated November 9, 1928. *Microfilm scan courtesy Southwest Collection, Texas Tech University.*

"Semper Fidelis" and "The Stars and Stripes Forever"—were performed during encores, along with a new "Golden Jubilee March."

Another facet of Sousa's appearance in Lubbock was a band competition held in between the two concerts. In the weeks before the event, Harry LeMaire, Texas Tech's director of bands, wrote letters and went to area towns to promote the upcoming competition. In the end, Lubbock High won the loving cup, which had been on display at Bowen's Drug Store advertising the entire spectacle. It was also reported that during intermissions, the Tech College Band performed under Sousa's direction.

Since that day in 1928, myths have persisted about the Sousa/South Plains connections. A plausible story is that Sousa visited Lubbock because of LeMaire—the two likely met while conducting military bands during the Spanish-American War, although this connection is difficult to corroborate. Stories also circulate about a piano owned by Sousa that was donated to the Museum of Texas Tech, as it was purportedly the instrument on which LeMaire and Sousa wrote music for the college, but museum staff confirm that no such piano appears in donation records.

Lubbock newspapers tell another connection that has not been authenticated and never came to fruition. The *Lubbock Morning Avalanche* reported that at one of the 1928 Lubbock concerts, Sousa promised Dr. Paul W. Horn (president of the college) that he would write a "Texas Tech March," something that could be seen in years to come as a "memento of an historic event." This was, unfortunately, not a terribly unique pledge; Sousa wrote for many universities in his later career, including the Universities of New Mexico, Nebraska, Illinois and Minnesota; Texas Women's University; and Marquette. But his vow to Tech was renewed on January 8, 1931, when a report in the *Morning Avalanche* explained that Sousa had almost completed his writing. This was followed on January 16 with a note that the march would be premiered at Spring Commencement. After that, the trail grows cold.

Sousa scholars explained to me that Sousa required prepurchasing copies of his marches to defray printing costs. Their archival records show that our young college was likely unable to procure enough funding, and so the "Sword of San Jacinto" march (which additionally might have been promised to another Texas ensemble at Fort Sam Houston) was retitled "Kansas Wildcats" for yet another school that was promised a Sousa march during the 1928 tour, Kansas State. That work, published in May 1931, was one of Sousa's last; he passed away in March 1932.

The LeMaire/Sousa ties gets further conflated with another fact: Texas Tech's current school song, "The Matador Song," was rewritten by LeMaire and premiered a few weeks after Sousa's composition was seemingly forgotten, at Spring Convocation on February 25, 1931.

In a 1975 interview housed at the Southwest Collection, former Texas Tech band member J. Culver Hill said that seeing Sousa's band in Lubbock was "the highlight of [his] life." Surely it was a wondrous thrill to see the invigorating "March King" on the dusty South Plains. Unfortunately, I have found no images of Sousa's brief Lubbock visit. Certainly, band members who were able to perform for Sousa had lasting memories of their experiences, as evidenced by the handful of Southwest Collection oral history interviews that recall that fateful November day. We may never fully know how or why or all the precise details of Sousa's connections to Texas Tech. But a small plaque on campus reminds us again how much history is hiding in plain sight.

VISITING THE GARDEN OF EDEN

Gene Lynskey

n Part I of this book, I wrote about my grandfather Courtney Sanders's discovery of a bison kill site in a canyon north of Slaton where he grew up. He later moved to Morton and raised his family, and that's where I grew up—out on a dusty farm northwest of town, just a few miles from the New Mexico state line.

My great-grandparents H.G. and Edith Sanders first lived in Young County and then in Floyd County, where they farmed and ranched before returning to North Texas in 1919. They followed the Burkburnett oil boom with a tent grocery store. But with a growing family, Edith insisted that they leave the lawless oil towns, so they moved in the early 1920s to civilization at Slaton, where they established the Texas Grocery Store on the town square. For their family of five children, they bought in the early 1930s an almost new home on West Garza Street, the house that we all would later love to visit.

For a young child like me, who grew up in the 1960s near Morton in a house in which sand sifted in every time the wind blew, the Sanders house in Slaton seemed so grand. It was a red-bricked bungalow with a beautiful red tile roof and a covered front porch with a swing. It had a musty basement and an old coal shoot with a furnace, which made a wonderful place to explore. The yard was covered in pecan, walnut, elm, apricot and even a

The H.G. and Edith Sanders home on West Garza in Slaton, circa 1940. *Courtesy Ann Murrah.*

magnolia tree that produced the biggest of blooms. In the back, there was a small rock-lined pond with goldfish and huge flower beds, as well as a garage with attached servant quarters. For me, it was a Garden of Eden.

Slaton also had sounds you would never hear on a cotton farm. You could stand outside and hear church bells ringing to let you know the time of day, and you could always hear the freight trains roaring through town.

I once got to spend the summer in the servant quarters behind the house. From there, it was an easy walk across the street to see another great-grandmother, Fannie Belle Green Teague. She was born in 1891 in North Texas and then moved with the family to a half-dugout in Indian Territory in 1899.

Then, in about 1909, when Fannie was about eighteen, the Greens moved to New Mexico to try homesteading. Meanwhile, the Santa Fe Railroad was completing a new Harvey House at nearby Vaughn, New Mexico, and a female railroad agent there soon recruited her to become a Harvey Girl at the new facility.

The Harvey Houses alongside the major railroad routes were probably the nation's first fast-food restaurants. Their prim and proper waitresses—the Harvey Girls—could take orders and serve their traveling guests within a few minutes while the train was loading water and fuel.

Fannie's work as a Harvey Girl led to her transfer to the new Harvey House in Slaton when it opened in 1912. Soon she met and married in 1915 Joe Teague Jr., the railroad's night ticket agent. In 1916, Joe and his father established a confectionery store that later became Teague Drug and operated in Slaton for sixty-six years until it closed in 1982. They raised three children.

Sometimes Fannie would drive me and my sisters, Donna and Elaine, to the drugstore in her 1957 Ford coupe. Even though she would be almost a block away, she would kill the engine and coast right up to the front of the store, sometimes running up on the curb and sidewalk. I guess she was trying to conserve gas like they did during the Depression and World War II. Then she would order us a cup of hot sweet limeade from the soda fountain and let us pick out a stack of comic books to take back to the house and read. I remember feeling guilty for not paying for comic books.

From the drugstore, Fannie would drive us to the railroad depot and park at the Harvey House where she worked more than fifty years before. We would watch the trains, which always stopped because Slaton was still a division point on the railroad. Then she headed back to her house along Railroad Avenue, which paralleled the train tracks.

What a treat to be chauffeured by this unique lady, who lived alongside Indians at the turn of the century, witnessed many wars, lived through the Great Depression and survived the Spanish flu epidemic of 1918–19. She once traveled in a covered wagon yet saw a man land on the moon. She was indeed a living history book.

I never knew my great-grandfathers H.G. Sanders and Joe Teague Jr. H.G. died in 1948 and Joe in 1961, when I was just a year old. Fortunately, I knew well my great-grandmothers: Edith Sanders, who lived in the glorious house on Garza until her death in 1980, and the ageless Fannie Teague, who lived right across the street until her death in 1992—one week shy of being 101. Both remained wise and alert until the very end.

Fannie's 100th birthday party in 1991 in Slaton was a wonderful celebration for our family. I shall always be grateful to that community for being a Garden of Eden for this country boy.

THE HISTORY BEHIND THE TAHOKA DAISY

Christena Stephens

T he first Texas native wildflower that became ingrained in my memory happened while working on trying to save a historical ranch headquarters. It was a little purple aster flower, a single-stem flower that sometimes grew in massive patches. Its growth pattern correlated with rainfall amounts during the year.

I went on to learn about more wildflowers thanks to Zoe Kirkpatrick's book *Wildflowers of the Western Plains: A Field Guide.* It indicates that the purple aster flower was the Tahoka Daisy, *Machaeranthera tanacetifolia,* or tansy aster. The next question was: how did such a small purple aster get the name of a small Texas town?

First, one needs to envision what the Llano Estacado once was, a vast prairie with hardly a tree in sight. Only a lone cholla cactus or a yucca in bloom broke the otherwise level landscape—perhaps similar to legendary Nessie of Loch Ness breaking the water with her head only to disappear again. The Llano Estacado was literally a waving sea of grass on land. As the area slowly developed, people and corporations moved in seeking fortune, and some were successful, such as cattlemen like C.C. Slaughter, David DeVitt and Cass Edwards.

One of the first things ranchers did was fence in their rangelands. They strung miles of barbed wire to keep their cattle at home and others out. Once the fences went up and the grazing began, the sea of grasses slowly

The Tahoka Daisy, which Effie Alley was reportedly growing on the Tahoka Lake Ranch around 1898. *Courtesy Christena Stephens.*

disappeared. In 1897, C.C. Slaughter purchased 1,600 acres at Tahoka Lake in Lynn County and leased the surrounding 140,000 acres. He then hired Jack Alley to run the ranch for him. Six years later, Slaughter sold the Tahoka Lake Ranch to Alley.

Alley's wife, Effie Paralee, participated in the ranching venture, helping work the cattle along with her husband and the cowboys. Reportedly, Effie was the first to discover a tiny purple aster flower growing at Tahoka Lake Ranch in 1898.

It took another twenty-five years for the purple aster to get noticed again, this time by Lubbock's Roberta Myrick. One day, while driving south of Lubbock on a dirt road, a lavender-colored flower caught her eye. It must have been a rainy season, for she said it was almost a shrub-like plant covered in purple flowers. Roberta got out of her car, dug up the daisy plant, took it back to Lubbock and planted it. As the plant went to seed, she saved the seeds and sent them to a Pennsylvania seed company, which in turn sent the seeds to New York. Eventually, the seeds ended up in the *Burpee Seed Catalog* around 1925.

Only a few details of Roberta's life are known, and no known photograph of her survives. But she was one of the first women in Lubbock County to own and drive her own car and was a charter member of the Lubbock Garden Club. Most importantly, she loved working with rare flowers. Roberta died at the age of eighty in 1948.

Because of Roberta's sharing the seeds, harvested near Tahoka, Texas, the flower became known as the Tahoka Daisy. It had been officially named by Carl Sigismund Kunth in 1832 as the prairie aster. Kunth was a German botanist who categorized and named a diversity of plants.

The Tahoka Daisy is a hardy, upright, sprawling annual native to the midwestern United States. It is quite easy to recognize by the dense, compact purple leaves, which are deeply divided into many narrow segments. It is an aster-family wildflower with two-inch lavender-blue flowers, a golden-yellow center and green, fern-like foliage. They prefer sandy or gravelly soil in full sun with a blooming period from May to September. It must have made a beautiful picture for Effie Alley while seeing the shimmering Tahoka Lake in the background.

LITTLE KNOWN, WIDELY KNOWN

LUBBOCK ARTIST BESS HUBBARD

Dolores Mosser

F ew people have heard of Bess Hubbard, but she was an internationally recognized award-winning artist who lived out her career in Lubbock.

From 1930 to 1950, Bess Hubbard "was probably the most progressive artist in Lubbock and a wide area of West Texas....She seems to have had an unrelenting thirst for new ideas and experiences," according to Peter Briggs, curator of art at the Museum of Texas Tech University. Briggs stated that the museum is always looking to add to its collection of more than one hundred pieces of Hubbard's works. Charles Adams, of the Charles Adam Art Gallery in Lubbock, treasures the Hubbard pieces he has in his collection, two studies of downtown Lubbock from the 1950s. Adams has also collected catalogues from past exhibits in which Bess Hubbard participated. Both he and Briggs gave glowing acknowledgements for a relatively unknown yet well-respected Lubbock artist.

Bess Bigham was born in 1896. She grew up in Fort Worth and attended Texas Christian University but found romance the summer of 1916 in Lubbock, Texas, while visiting her cousin when she met a young farmer, Chester A. Hubbard, who also worked for a local car dealership. The couple married the following year, made their home in Lubbock and became the parents of one son.

Perhaps it was the wide open spaces of the Llano Estacado that inspired Bess's love for art and the development of a progressive style as she took up art as a hobby. By 1925, Hubbard's "hobby" had developed into a distinctive format that included painting, printmaking and sculpture. Later, she studied art at the University of New Mexico, Colorado College, Bradley University and the Chicago Academy of Fine Arts.

Taking advantage of several famous art instructors, Bess and her work soon developed a following. According to the *Handbook of Texas*, she "won notice for her impressionist-style paintings, lithographs, and etchings featuring local subjects and southwestern regional motifs."

By the 1940s, Hubbard had embraced a sculpting technique of William Zorach, a noted American sculptor, who taught at the Art Student League in New York City. Both artists used "direct-method carving" over traditional methods of casting. According to the *Handbook*, "She concentrated on giving her pieces prominent features and distinct lines of character, frequently combining rough, and polished, surfaces for textural interest."

Hubbard was always moving forward into new artistic mediums. She sought out Taos Indians to use as her models and later took an interest in designing jewelry and stained glass.

National admiration for her art developed during the 1950s. Her works were exhibited at Southern Methodist University, Hardin-Simmons University, the Museum of Fine Arts in Little Rock, the Seattle Art Museum, the Los Angeles County Art Institute, the Argent Gallery in New York, the Dallas Museum of Art, the Museum of Fine Art in Houston, the Witte Museum in San Antonio, the Schleier Galleries in Denver, the Colorado Springs Art Institute, the Denver Art Museum, the School of American Research Museum in Santa Fe and, of course, the Museum of Texas Tech University in Lubbock.

Hubbard also was featured in international showings in various museums and galleries in Europe. Her two best-known sculptures, *La Reboza* (1952) and *Green Goddess* (1949), were featured in *LIFE* magazine and *Harper's Bazaar* in the mid-1950s.

Over the next twenty years, Hubbard received awards from the National Gallery of Design, Metroplex Museum, Argent Gallery, Honolulu Academy of Art, Laguna Beach Art Association, Dallas Museum of Fine Arts and at the Fort Worth Annual Texas Print Exhibition.

Hubbard was active in many art associations and helped to encourage many young artists. Locally, she attended the First Christian Church, worked as a counselor for the Boy Scouts and served on the South Plains Art Guild and the Mural Committee of the West Texas Museum Association.

After Chester's death in 1957, she once again found a new form of art to explore. She began casting small works in bronze and chrome and restored

Memorial carved by Bess Hubbard and after her death and placed at her grave in the Hubbard family plot, Lubbock City Cemetery. *Courtesy Dolores Mosser.*

the 1930 murals in the lobby of the old Caprock Hotel in Lubbock. As a gift to her family, she carved a monument to stand over their graves. Later, she cast bronze sculptures of her son and two grandchildren that were exhibited in London.

Bess died at her home in Lubbock on March 23, 1977, and was buried in her family's plot at the City of Lubbock Cemetery. Her work is in the permanent collections of the Texas Tech Museum, the Dallas Museum of Art, the Texas Fine Arts Association, the Elisabet Ney Museum and the Colorado Springs Fine Arts Center.

HAROLD D. BUGBEE, ARTIST AND ILLUSTRATOR OF WIDE RENOWN

Michael R. Grauer

One of the most prolific artists of the Panhandle and South Plains regions was Harold Dow Bugbee (1900–1963). A landscape, genre and portrait painter, as well as an illustrator, muralist, graphic artist and sculptor, Bugbee left a lasting legacy of art that helped define the history of the Llano Estacado.

At the suggestion of his cousin, cattleman T.S. Bugbee, Harold came to the Texas Panhandle from Lexington, Massachusetts, in 1914 with his parents, Charles H. and Grace Dow Bugbee. He attended high school at Clarendon and, showing an interest in sketching, studied architectural drawing at Texas Agricultural and Mechanical College (now Texas A&M University) in 1917.

To further his art education, in 1919 he traveled to Taos, New Mexico, seeking instruction from W. Herbert Dunton, one of the founding members of the Taos Society of Artists and an artist he admired greatly. Although he did not receive any instruction from Dunton, they remained friends until Dunton's death in 1936. Following the advice of Bert Geer Phillips, another Taos "founder," Bugbee enrolled at the Cumming School of Art in Des Moines, Iowa, in 1920.

After two years of academic study at Cumming, Bugbee returned to Texas and refocused on the Old West. Under the watchful eyes of his uncle and cattlemen Frank Collinson and Charles Goodnight, Bugbee sketched the landscape and wildlife of the Texas Panhandle, Indians and cowboys and

H.D. Bugbee's first sketch of a covered wagon for the cover of the *Panhandle-Plains Historical Review* (1930); his work would appear on thirty-three consecutive annual issues.

nostalgic scenes of the Panhandle-Plains frontier. Each fall, from 1922 until the late 1930s, Bugbee traveled to Taos to paint with his fellow artists "Buck" Dunton, Frank Hoffman, Leon Gaspard and Ralph Meyers, often packing into the mountains to paint with either Meyers or Dunton.

By the early 1930s, galleries in New York, Denver, Chicago and Kansas City were handling Bugbee's work. He also found work as an illustrator, working for "pulps" and "slicks." In 1933, Bugbee began illustrating for magazines such as *Ranch Romances, Western Stories, Country Gentleman* and *Field and Stream*, as well as books on western history including J. Evetts Haley's *Charles Goodnight: Cowman and Plainsman*, Willie N. Lewis's *Between Sun and Sod*, S. Omar Barker's *Songs of the Saddleman*, Eugene Manlove Rhodes's *The Little World Waddies* and others. Additionally, Bugbee illustrated many Texas newspapers. He also illustrated the front cover of the *Panhandle-Plains Historical Review* from 1930 through 1962. All the while, Bugbee continued to make easel paintings.

Bugbee exhibited first in the Texas Panhandle in the late 1920s in Amarillo and Dalhart, then at the Tri-State Fair at Amarillo, the Fort Worth Frontier Centennial Exposition in 1936, the Greater Texas and Pan-American Exposition at Dallas in 1937 (in the Hall of State) and in the annual West Texas art exhibitions at Fort Worth. He also had numerous solo exhibitions all over Texas and exhibited at Taos.

Bugbee designed the bronze bas relief for the trail-drives monument near Vernon, Texas, in 1931 and then began painting murals. Under the Public Works of Art Project (1934), he painted the first of five murals for Pioneer Hall at the Panhandle-Plains Historical Museum.

After being drafted into the U.S. Army in 1942 (at age forty-two), Bugbee quickly completed murals for the Old Tascosa supper club in Amarillo's Herring Hotel. Following his discharge, he painted three murals for the Amarillo Army Air Field, two of which are now in the Smithsonian American Art Museum.

Bugbee became Panhandle-Plains Historical Museum's first paid curator of art in 1951, agreeing to work part time so he could continue painting. He painted seventeen murals of American Indian life for the museum's former Indian Hall, and in 1958, he finished the mural *Working Cattle on the Open Range* in Pioneer Hall.

Known primarily for his pen-and-ink and ink drybrush drawings used to illustrate pulp magazines, Bugbee's skills as a draftsman are widely praised. In fact, Jeff Dykes included him in his seminal biographical dictionary, *Fifty Great Western Illustrators*, based almost exclusively on Bugbee's skill with ink.

However, he was equally skilled in graphite and charcoal, as well as lithographic crayon on pebbled paper. Bugbee also showed great control and spontaneity in watercolor, using either washes or brushstrokes to master this most unforgiving of media. Unknown to most are Bugbee's works in colored pencil. Unsatisfied with colored pencils as color fillers, he showed immense verve in his pencil strokes, allowing the medium to flow and express, almost like a liquid medium. Moreover, Bugbee experimented successfully in color oil pastels, using them much as he had colored pencil.

Today, more than 2,500 Bugbee works, a reconstruction of his studio and a gallery dedicated to his work are part of the Panhandle-Plains Historical Museum's art collection. Bugbee's works are fitting tribute to his devotion to the Panhandle-Plains region of Texas and the greater Southwest.

Bugbee's work can also be found at the Smithsonian American Art Museum; the Montana Historical Society, Helena, Montana; the Amon Carter Museum, Fort Worth; the Cattleman's Museum, Fort Worth; American Quarter Horse Heritage Center and Museum, Amarillo, Texas; Saint's Roost Museum, Clarendon, Texas; the Red River Valley Museum, Vernon, Texas; the National Ranching Heritage Center, Lubbock; Museum of the Southwest, Midland, Texas; the National Cowboy & Western Heritage Museum, Oklahoma City; the Gilcrease Museum, Tulsa; and the J. Evetts Haley History Center, Midland, Texas.

Texas A&M University Press published the first monograph on the artist, *Making a Hand: The Art of H.D. Bugbee,* in September 2019.

BEHIND THE IRON GATES

THE SOUTHWEST COLLECTION AT TEXAS TECH UNIVERSITY

David J. Murrah

Many of the essays in this book, almost all of which were selected from the "Caprock Chronicles" series that began in the Sunday issues of the *Lubbock Avalanche-Journal* in 2016, were written by scholars, many of whom made use of the resources of one of the nation's premier research centers, the Southwest Collection/Special Collections Library at Texas Tech University.

Although it was not created as a separate entity until 1955, the Southwest Collection dates to the early beginnings of Texas Tech. Its genesis grew out of the combined enthusiasm of several young historians who in the mid-1920s were trying to preserve the recent, rich and colorful history of West Texas. In 1924, Rupert N. Richardson of Hardin-Simmons University in Abilene collaborated with William Curry Holden, who was then at cross-town McMurry College, to create the West Texas Historical Association, which then published an annual historical *Year Book*. Three years later, J. Evetts Haley on behalf of the Panhandle-Plains Historical Society, began a similar project, the *Panhandle-Plains Historical Review*.

Both journals offered a ready forum for the abundant stories on the development of the region. Meanwhile, in 1929, Texas Tech acquired from Clifford B. Jones of the Spur Ranch more than twenty-six thousand pages of the ranch's earliest records, a resource that became the heart of the future Southwest Collection. The following year, Holden, who had moved to Tech in 1929, teamed with his former student and Tech history instructor H. Bailey Carroll to solicit and collect the early records of the Scottish-owned Matador Land and Cattle Company. Both collections were housed in the Texas Tech Library under the control of its librarian, Elizabeth Howard West. When Tech built a new library in 1938, Miss West placed the collection behind two sets of iron gates.

Unfortunately, after Miss West retired in 1942, her immediate successors had little regard for old records and threw away some of them, including some old newspapers tossed by new librarian A.S. Gaylord in 1948. When Dr. Holden, who had become chair of the history department, discovered the papers in the trash, he promptly called on Gaylord and quickly "converted" the librarian to a new appreciation of history.

The incident prompted Holden to seek college and community support to create a permanent repository for Tech's accumulated historical documents. In the spring of 1948, Lubbock attorney George Dupree hosted at his home both college officials and community historical leaders and discussed a concept of a major historical research center; he suggested that it be called the Southwest Collection.

Soon after the meeting, Texas Tech Library director Gaylord pulled together all southwestern materials and assigned them to the northeast corner of the library behind a set of iron gates, the place that Tech's first librarian, Elizabeth Howard West, had also designated for a special collection. However, support for growth did not immediately develop.

Then, in 1951, Texas Tech hired its first of several distinguished professors, Carl Coke Rister, a historian who had written ten major studies on the American Southwest at the University of Oklahoma, and asked him to help develop the Southwest Collection. At the same time, Holden, new Tech librarian Ray Janeway and history professor Ernest Wallace developed a promotional brochure in which Holden noted that "the Southwest Collection will in time make Texas Technological College famous as a research center."

Ironically, it was Carl Coke Rister's death in the spring of 1955 that created new life for the Southwest Collection. His wife, Mattie, offered to sell to Texas Tech her husband's vast library and collection of southwestern material. On May 15, longtime proponents W.C. Holden, Ray Janeway, George Dupree and Clifford B. Jones met with the new Tech president E.N. Jones and the newest member of the Tech Board of Directors, J. Evetts Haley, and the group decided to ask the board to create the Southwest Collection as a separate department of the college and to house it in the museum.

The iconic iron gates, to the left of the students in picture on left, were once a part of Texas Tech's first library building and became the gateway to the Southwest Collection in 1948. Fifty years later, they made the move to the new Southwest Collection/Special Collections Library, which opened in 1998. *Courtesy Lynn Whitfield and the University Archives, Southwest Collection, Texas Tech University.*

Haley then carried the proposal to the board, and in addition, he recommended that the college employ former Texas State archivist Seymour V. Connor as its first full-time director. The board agreed and established a modest $14,000 budget for the new Southwest Collection. On September 1, 1955, Connor moved the library's books and research materials to a classroom in the West Texas Museum (now Holden Hall), and the Southwest Collection opened as a fully integrated research center.

As Texas Tech grew, so did the Southwest Collection. In 1962, Tech built a new library and gave a sizeable portion of the old building to the Southwest Collection in what is now the Mathematics Building. There it secured the four-level stack area for storage and made use of the adjacent paneled reading rooms, the same area that Tech's first librarian, Elizabeth Howard West, had created with the iron gates.

In 1963, Roy Sylvan Dunn became the second director of the Southwest Collection and soon established a full-time field program that led to the collecting of millions of historical documents and hundreds of newspapers and oral histories. By the 1980s, the repository had outgrown its facility, but by the mid-1990s, under the guidance of its third director, David J. Murrah (1977–96), funding had been secured for the present Southwest Collection/Special Collections Library, which opened in 1997. It has become one of the largest centers of its kind in the nation.

The same iron gates Miss West designed to be the entrance to the historical research center in 1938 now frame the formal entry of the reading room of the Southwest Collection. They stand as a tribute to Texas Tech's more than ninety years of collecting and preserving historical material. These resources became the basis for the production of thousands of theses, dissertations, books and journal, magazine and newspaper articles—including, of course, a great number of the more than two hundred essays that have been a part of the "Caprock Chronicles" series.

SELECTED BIBLIOGRAPHY

Abbe, Donald, Paul H. Carlson, and David J. Murrah. *Lubbock and the South Plains: An Illustrated History*. 2nd ed. Tarzana, CA: Preferred Marketing, 1995.

Blodgett, Jan. *Land of Bright Promise: Advertising the Texas Panhandle and South Plains, 1870–1917*. Austin: University of Texas Press, 1988.

Carlson, Paul H. *Amarillo: The Story of a Western Town*. Lubbock: Texas Tech University Press, 2006.

———. *The Buffalo Soldier Tragedy of 1877*. College Station: Texas A&M University Press, 2003.

———. *Deep Time and the Texas High Plains: History & Geology*. Lubbock: Texas Tech University Press, 2005.

———. *Empire Builder in the Texas Panhandle: William Henry Bush*. College Station: Texas Tech University Press, 1996.

Carlson, Paul H., and Bruce Glasrud, eds. *West Texas: A History of the Giant Side of the State*. Norman: University of Oklahoma Press, 2014.

Carlson, Paul H., and David J. Murrah, eds. *Hidden History of the Llano Estacado*. Charleston, SC: The History Press, 2017.

Fleming, Elvis E., and David J. Murrah. *Texas' Last Frontier: A New History of Cochran County*. Morton, TX: Cochran County Historical Commission, 2001.

Glasrud, Bruce, and Paul H. Carlson, with Tai D. Kreidler, eds. *Slavery to Integration: Black Americans in West Texas*. Abilene, TX: State House Press, 2007.

Gracy, David B., II. *A Man Absolutely Sure of Himself: Texan George Washington Littlefield*. Norman: University of Oklahoma Press, 2019.

Grauer, Michael R. *Littlefield Lands: Colonization on the Texas Plains, 1912–1920*. Austin: University of Texas Press, 1968.

———. *Making a Hand: The Art of H.D. Bugbee*. College Station: Texas A&M University Press, 2020.

Haley, J. Evetts. *Charles Goodnight: Cowman and Plainsman*. Boston: Houghton Mifflin Company, 1936.

———. *The XIT Ranch of Texas and the Early Days of the Llano Estacado*. Garden City, NY: Doubleday, 1976.

Hamalainnen, Pekka. *The Comanche Empire*. New Haven, CT: Yale University Press, 2008.

Holiday, Vance T. *Paleoindian Geoarchaeology of the Southern High Plains*. Foreword by Thomas R. Hester. Austin: University of Texas Press, 1997.

Hunt, George M. *Early Days Upon the Plains of Texas*. Lubbock, TX: Avalanche Publishing Company, 1919.

Kenner, Charles L. *The Comanchero Frontier: A History of New Mexican-Plains Indian Relations*. Norman: University of Oklahoma Press, 1994.

Morris, John Miller. *El Llano Estacado: Exploration and Imagination on the High Plains of Texas and New Mexico, 1536–1860*. Austin: Texas State Historical Association, 1997.

Murrah, David J. *"And Are We Yet Alive?": A History of the Northwest Texas Conference of the United Methodist Church*. Foreword by Bishop D. Max Whitfield. Buffalo Gap, TX: State House Press, 2009.

———. *C.C. Slaughter: Rancher, Banker, Baptist*. Austin: University of Texas Press, 1981.

———. *Oil, Taxes, and Cats: A History of the Devitt Family and the Mallet Ranch*. Lubbock: Texas Tech University Press, 1994.

Murrah, David J., and Paul H. Carlson. *Historic Tales of the Llano Estacado*. Charleston, SC: The History Press, 2020.

Rathjen, Fred. *The Texas Panhandle Frontier*. Revised ed. Introduction by Elmer Kelton. Lubbock: Texas Tech University Press, 1998.

Robinson, Sherry. *I Fought the Good Fight: A History of the Lipan Apaches*. Denton: University of North Texas Press, 2013.

Siemens, Tina (Katharina). *Seminole: Some People Never Give Up*. N.p.: independently published, 2019.

INDEX

T

ABOUT THE CONTRIBUTORS

DONALD ABBE, PhD, is former curator of history at the Silent Wings Museum in Lubbock and historian of the Llano Estacado.

AUSTIN ALLISON, MA, is a cataloguing supervisor for the Southwest Collection/Special Collections Library at Texas Tech.

H. ALLEN ANDERSON, PhD, is a senior archival associate and historian for the Southwest Collection/Special Collections Library at Texas Tech, where he is currently transcribing oral histories of the American Southwest.

PAUL H. CARLSON, PhD, is Professor of History Emeritus at Texas Tech University and author of more than twenty books on the history of the American Southwest.

CLINT CHAMBERS, MD, is a retired physician with a longtime interest in the Santa Fe Trail and its little-known branches that coursed the Texas Panhandle.

PAUL CHAPLO, MA, earned his master's degree in photography from Rochester Institute of Technology and works as a professional aerial and energy sector photographer based in Texas.

ABOUT THE CONTRIBUTORS

Sandy Fortenberry is the chair of the Lubbock County Historical Commission.

Michael R. Grauer is the McCasland Chair of Cowboy Culture/curator of Cowboy Collections and Western Art at the National Cowboy & Western Heritage Museum in Oklahoma City. His book, *Making a Hand: The Art of H.D. Bugbee*, was based on his thirty-one years of research on Mr. Bugbee while serving as curator of art and western heritage at Panhandle-Plains Historical Museum at Canyon, Texas, from 1987 to 2018.

Monica Hightower has been a chuck wagon owner and specialty caterer for fifteen years.

Jorge Iber, PhD, specializes in the history of Latinos in U.S. sport history and is associate dean at the College of Arts and Sciences and a professor in the Department of History at Texas Tech University.

Marty Kuhlman, PhD, is a professor of history at West Texas A&M University in Canyon, Texas.

Gene Lynskey is a hunting guide and farmer and lives in Cochran County near Morton, Texas.

Dolores Mosser is a children book's author and historian of the western Llano Estacado and lives in Lubbock.

Richard Peterson, PhD, is a Professor Emeritus of Atmospheric Sciences at Texas Tech University.

Sherry Robinson is an award-winning journalist and author and longtime resident of Albuquerque, New Mexico.

Cameron L. Saffel, PhD, is an associate professor of heritage and museum sciences and curator of history for the Museum of Texas Tech University.

Tina (Katharina) Siemens immigrated to the United States in 1977 and owns and operates JW&T Construction in Seminole, Texas, with her husband, John Siemens.

ABOUT THE CONTRIBUTORS

JENNIFER SPURRIER is an associate archivist at the Southwest Collection/Special Collections Library.

CHRISTENA STEPHENS is a writer, fine-art photographer, nonprofit geek and outdoor enthusiast living in Sundown, Texas.

ELISSA STROMAN is a musicologist, oral historian and archivist based in Lubbock, Texas; since 2010, she has overseen the audio/visual and oral history holdings of the Southwest Collection/Special Collections Library at Texas Tech University.

JEAN A. STUNTZ, PhD, is a professor of history at West Texas A&M University in Canyon.

SCOTT WHITE, PhD, is native West Texan who spent several years in construction before moving into museum work at Texas Tech University

B. LYNN WHITFIELD is the university archivist for Texas Tech University, associate director for the West Texas Historical Association and a member of the executive board for the Lubbock Heritage Society.

ABOUT THE EDITORS

JOHN T. "JACK" BECKER is a retired librarian from Texas Tech University and the current editor of "Caprock Chronicles," a weekly newspaper column that appears every Sunday in the *Lubbock Avalanche-Journal*. He has authored and coauthored several book and journal articles on various topics pertaining to the history of West Texas. A native of Kentucky, he now lives with his wife, Cindy, in Lubbock "west of town."

DAVID J. MURRAH, PhD, is a museum and historical consultant. He served for twenty-five years as archivist and director of the Southwest Collection at Texas Tech University before entering the museum exhibit/design field with Southwest Museum Services of Houston. He has written or edited eleven books and numerous articles on Texas history and is a Fellow of both the Texas State Historical Association and the West Texas Historical Association. A native of the high plains (Gruver, Texas), he and his wife, Ann, now live on the Texas coastal plains at Rockport.

Visit us at
www.historypress.com